Your Land, My Land

Your Land, My Land
Children in the Process of Acculturation

Jacklyn Blake Clayton

Heinemann
Portsmouth, NH

Heinemann
A division of Reed Elsevier Inc.
361 Hanover Street
Portsmouth, NH 03801-3912
Offices and agents throughout the world

Every effort has been made to contact the copyright holders for permission to reprint borrowed material where necessary. We regret any oversights that may have occurred and would be happy to rectify them in future printings of this work.

The names of all participants—students, families, teachers, schools, and the city—have been changed to preserve their anonymity.

"This Land is Your Land," words and music by Woodie Guthrie. TRO-©-Copyright 1956 (Renewed) 1958 (Renewed) 1970 Ludlow Music, Inc., New York, New York. Used by permission.

Library of Congress Cataloging-in-Publication Data
Clayton, Jacklyn Blake.
  Your land, my land: children in the process of acculturation / Jacklyn Blake Clayton.
    p.   cm.
  Includes bibliographical references.
  ISBN 0–435–08852–1
  1. Students. Foreign—United States—Case studies.
  2. Acculturation—United States—Case studies.   I.   Title.
  LC3731.C555   1995
  371.8'22'0973—dc20   95–37843
                                                        CIP

Editor: Carolyn Coman
Cover design and illustration: Gwen Frankfeldt
Printed in the United States of America on acid free paper
99   98   97   96   95   DA   1   2   3   4   5   6   7   8   9

To the memory of my late parents, Everett (Jack) and Lynda Blake, who started me on the journey of biculturalism,

To my husband and children, Paul, John, and Cathryn, who unceasingly supported, celebrated, and occasionally endured my continuing cross-cultural pilgrimage, and

To all, especially teachers, who help cross-cultural children claim the richness of their heritage.

Contents

Acknowledgments

Deep and special thanks go to the children and families who allowed me into their lives during a very vulnerable time. Without their candor and trust, this book could not have been written. To the teachers, the principals, and the public school system of Winsted, I also express my appreciation for access to their classrooms, and, to the teachers particularly, heartfelt gratitude for their willingness to share their experiences with me despite the daily pressures of school and the particular pressures of the work-to-rule action they had undertaken. In addition, this book would not have been possible without the translators who gave generously of their time and their abilities.

There are numerous others who have been instrumental in the production of this book: Jeanne Paratore's enthusiasm and insistence pushed me to investigate the possibility of publication; Keith McClelland helped in the technical production of the paradigm; Marilyn Crocker perceptively untangled an editing block; our children, John and Cathy, offered technical and psychological support; Carolyn Coman, editor at Heinemann, had a vision and encouraged my efforts all along the way. I am deeply grateful to them all.

Most of all, to my husband, who has very genially and generously shared, suffered, and rejoiced through the process of my doctorate as well as the editing of this book, I owe gratitude deeper than words can express.

Your Land, My Land

[B]urning with curiosity, [Alice] ran across the field after [the rab-bit], and was just in time to see it pop down a large rabbit hole un-der the hedge. In another moment down went Alice after it . . .

[S]he had plenty of time as she went down to look about her, and to wonder what was going to happen next. First she tried to look down and make out what she was coming to, but it was too dark to see anything; then she looked at the sides . . . and noticed that they were filled with cupboards and bookshelves; here and there she saw maps and pictures hung upon pegs. . . . Down, down, down. Would the fall never come to an end? . . . Down, down, down. . . . [S]uddenly, thump! thump! down she came upon a heap of sticks and dry leaves, and the fall was over . . .

[S]he walked . . . wondering how she was ever to get out again. Suddenly, she came upon a . . . tiny golden key . . . Alice's first idea was that this might belong to one of the doors . . . but alas! either the locks were too large, or the key was too small . . . However, on the second time round . . . she tried the little golden key in the lock, and to her great delight it fitted!

—Lewis Carroll, *Alice in Wonderland*

"Where do you come from? Where are you going?"

Munching on a sandwich at lunch time, Sally, the first grade teacher, looked at me, "Can I interrupt your lunch long enough to talk about Yoshio?" Yoshio was one of my ESL students from Japan; he had been in her class for two weeks. Learning English was not easy for him. Before I could answer, she continued, "I just do not know how to reach him. Yesterday morning I gave him some seat work—some of the things you and I talked about that he could do—and he would not sit at his desk and get it done. He kept hanging around other kids' desks, which made it hard for them. Then, after lunch when it was time to come back to the classroom, he wrapped himself around a pole in the lunch room and would not let go. It took the principal and the guidance counselor and me to loosen him from the pole and march him upstairs. It's like he's from a different planet. What's going on? I really don't understand. I wish you could keep him in your class longer than just that one period until he can learn to talk a little and act like the other kids in the class." (Field notes, November 8, 1989)

1

THIS INCIDENT WAS ONE OF MANY THAT PROPELLED ME FROM TEACHER TO doctoral student after 15 years of teaching English as a Second Language (ESL). It seemed to me that as more and more non–English-speaking children enter mainstream classrooms in the United States, their mainstream teachers will need to become aware of not only what their students are experiencing, but also how teaching strategies and classroom assumptions may affect those who come from different cultures with different values. Because non-European immigrants will be in significantly higher numbers than European immigrants during the 1990s, the children of all these diverse nationals will not naturally share many of the Anglo-European cultural orientations on which the United States is based. And yet, most teachers are surprised when these children do not "fit in" with a fair amount of ease. The demographic fact of the influx of many nationalities provides new challenges to the educational systems of U.S. cities and towns and villages, not only for ESL and bilingual programs, but also for mainstream teachers.

This book is based on the data collected for my doctoral dissertation. As the study progressed, I became aware that there were other reasons for this exploration: one personal, the other professional. It became clear to me that perhaps there had been an underlying interest in this issue for much longer than I realized. The daughter of missionary educators, I was born and grew up in Turkey, coming to the United States for the first time when I was in the first grade. Despite the fact that Turkish was the first language I *spoke*, my parents and other USAmerican teachers in the school always spoke to me in English; hence I grew up with fluency in both languages and cultures. I completed grades two through five at a Turkish primary school, but my education from sixth grade on was in English. Hence, coming to the United States for first and eighth grades, and later to complete high school and college, was not a linguistic issue for me, although learning to be a student in an Anglo-American school continued to undefinably haunt me, even through college and beyond.

Professionally, for twelve years a colleague and I were "the ESL program" in a suburban school system with a foreign student population small enough not to warrant a bilingual program. Our ESL classes were small, pull-out, grade-and-ability grouped, and a multicultural mix from all corners of the globe. In addition to teaching the students, we also would meet with their mainstream classroom teachers to try to facilitate and maximize the teaching/learning process. Many of the questions addressed to me at the time naturally were about the linguistic development of the students. I found my responses incorporating not only theories of language development but also my instincts about the cultural adjustment that I felt the children were experiencing. I decided that I wanted to find out directly from children about the challenges they felt in addition to learning the language.

Hence, this is the story of four newly arrived, non–English-speaking children in grades 4 through 6 in a suburban school system. I followed them for their first three months in school, looking at the process of their adjustment from their perspective and asking how the school and teacher impacted that adjustment. My focus centered around two primary questions: Was there some kind of underlying pattern of acculturation that the four students shared, and what was the role of the school and the classroom teacher in that process of acculturation?

Erik was from Norway, in grade 4, here for a period of a year while his father did postgraduate work at a university; Carina was from Brazil, in grade 5, here for two years with her business executive father and family; Yevgeny, from Russia, also in grade 5, had just emigrated with his brother and biologist mother; and Raina, from Bulgaria, in grade 6, had come with her younger sister to join her mother and father who had emigrated before their children. Obviously, these were children of families who had come here voluntarily, families who had decided that relocation in the United States was desirable or necessary for them. The immigrant families came for political and/or economic reasons; the sojourners, for educational and/or business reasons.

Aged 9 to 11 years, the four children were in three different schools; they were all newly arrived, and their exposure to English was nonexistent to minimal. By parental choice or default, they were all in ESL programs (vis-a-vis bilingual programs).

EVEN THOUGH THE FOCUS WAS ON CHILDREN, THEIR TEACHERS AND PARENTS were also participants in this study. The teachers were dedicated, caring individuals who wanted very much to understand and help these newcomers. The teachers' well-meaning strategies, their hopes, their victories, as well as their frustrations, were shared with me along with assumptions so endemic that they were not aware they had them. They saw these students as eventual assets to their classrooms, but often felt stymied in their efforts to help them. The parents of these children, despite having to learn new ways themselves, were very supportive of the experience their children were having. They were also very interested in my study and eager to be of help, even though they were in a brand new country and culture.

My experience as an ESL teacher also focused the time limits of the study: from September to December. I had noticed that the first three months in our schools were crucial in these children's lives. It was during this time that they did not have the language to understand others or to express themselves. It was during this time that they were trying to get a grasp of the explicit routines and implicit guidelines of the class. What were the routines that puzzled them? How did they make sense out of the chaos that surrounded them? Did they experience highs and lows in any pattern? How did they go about making friends?

Because the students were newly arrived, in order to get their perspective on what was happening to them, it was necessary to be able to speak with them in their own languages. Translators were used whose first language was the home language of each student. The same translators were used also with the parents; it was not assumed that the parents could speak English. The translators also helped to validate information about their culture; they were another source of understanding the cultural background of the student. They had first-hand knowledge of the participant's culture, but were sufficiently removed from it to offer objectivity and reflection. They were able to add amplification or clarification to issues or behaviors within the school context that seemed ambiguous even after consultation with the primary participants (student and/or parent). In the stories, they are referred to as T/EI (Translator/Ethnic Informant).

Although the translators contributed tangentially, the primary information that creates the stories came from four different sources: students, teachers, parents, and myself. At the prestudy interview with all the families and teachers, my requests were spelled out: The students were asked to keep a journal and to participate in interviews every two weeks with me and the translator; the parents and teachers were asked to do the same, with interviews every three weeks with the teachers and every four weeks with the parents. Finally, I was a participant/observer in the classes for the three months of the study. In that role, I was a participant only at times when I felt that it would not interfere with the initiatives of the teacher, peers, or ESL specialist. With these four different sources, incidents that came up could often have more than one perspective, a fact that proved to be invaluable in many ways and made for a richer understanding of the process. Because I was curious about whether my presence affected the students in any way, I checked with the teachers as well as with the families for their thoughts. Most of them said that they felt it made no difference; one teacher commented that she did not think the children were aware that I was observing them; another felt that the cross-cultural student attempted more interaction with the teacher when I was in the room.

A LITTLE BACKGROUND INFORMATION IS USEFUL IN THINKING ABOUT THESE CROSS-cultural students and their stories.

> Of course the first thing to do was to make a grand survey of the country she was going to travel through. "It's something very like learning geography," thought Alice, as she stood on tiptoe in hopes of being able to see further.
>
> —Lewis Carroll, *Through the Looking Glass*

Despite the fact that people have been living in cross-cultural contexts for almost 5000 years, models, theories, and even definitions that describe the process of adjustment to life in a different land are not yet systematized. Furthermore, there is a distinct difference between the *process* and the *state* of acculturation. The process elicits a variety of strategies from the newcomer in an effort to feel comfortable in the new environment. The state is the end of the journey. This book is about the *process*.

The traditional view of acculturation is the assimilation of minority ethnic people into the majority context; that is, in the United States, they become "Americanized." In this view, which suggests a linear adjustment, there seems to be a series of phases that the foreigner experiences: The phases begin with preparation and entry into the new culture, at which point the feelings are normal to high; a second phase, in which the foreigner is a spectator, wherein emotions vary from mostly high to very low; a third phase, in which increased participation makes the foreigner realize the magnitude of the differences between the host culture and home culture, which in turn starts a downward trend in emotional well-being; a fourth phase of shock, wherein the emotions are very negative. Then the adaptation (fifth) phase begins, in which the emotions return closer to normal as the foreigner learns to function in the host country. The end of the process is characterized by the minority person or group giving up its traditions, values, and language, and replacing them with those of the majority culture.

Generally, because the end goal of this unidirectional model is assimilation, there is not room for variation in response, only greater and lesser degrees of assimilation. This is problematic for those who believe that people from other cultures can have a beneficial impact on the host or dominant culture, that there can be a give-and-take between the two for the enrichment of all.

A more recent view of acculturation is a multidimensional pattern, which suggests a variety of end-states. Assimilation may be one of the responses, but another may also be one of integration, separation, or marginalization (Berry, Kim, and Boski, 1988). In assimilation, the newcomer becomes one with the new culture, taking on the values, language, and traditions of the new culture; in integration, the newcomer is able to integrate both cultures into his or her life, to make a contribution to the host community as well as to be affected by it. Marginalization refers to the opposite of integration, wherein the newcomer no longer feels comfortable in either culture. Separation occurs when, for any number of reasons, the person withdraws and strengthens ties with the old culture.

People may use different strategies during the acculturation process. Three of these strategies are adjustment, reaction, or withdrawal (Berry et al., 1988). Each of these strategies is in response to the conflict created by the contact with the new culture: Adjustment and withdrawal reduce conflict in diametrically opposed ways; reaction retaliates against it. People who use adjustment are those who respond to the stress of the conflict by changing their behavior, trying to fit in with the environment. On the other hand, the response to the conflict may be that of withdrawal, in which the person moves away from the conflict situation in order to alleviate the stress and achieve some kind of congruence. Finally, there may be a strong reaction to the conflict, which is reduced by changing the context, not the person's behavior.

Both teachers and students are impacted during the process by how they view the desired end-state. A teacher assuming assimilation will use (consciously or unconsciously) different strategies than one assuming integration. For example, with integration in mind, *differences* that the cross-cultural student brings will not mean *deficiencies* to be addressed, but rather *distinctions* to be celebrated. A student determined (consciously or unconsciously) not to make the most of the move will thwart all efforts by others toward friendship.

Children bring some special issues to the process of acculturation. Usually they have not had a say in the decision to make the move; often the move may resemble an uprooting wherein all that is familiar, that gives meaning to self as well as surroundings, is lost. The motivation factor for the children is survival in the context in which they find themselves. Cross-cultural children who are not in bilingual programs (by choice or default) have little reference group support in school. In many classrooms, particularly in low-incidence populations, they are the only ones in the whole school who may be from a foreign country. In these same school systems, the attitudes of the administration and the teachers help create the climate of the school as either hostile or open to children from other countries. Cross-cultural students will adjust their responses according to their perceptions of the situation, with perceived hostility producing more primary group cohesion and amity producing more openness to the new culture, as corroborated by Sung (1987). Mainstream teachers play a crucial role in this process during the first few months of acculturation.

FOR A PARTICULAR CULTURE TO SURVIVE, IT MUST BE PASSED ON FROM GENERATION TO generation. In families, the newborn and the young are socialized into the values and behaviors of their parents and grandparents. As children leave the security of their homes to start their formal education, the school is charged with the responsibility of further socialization during the many hours the children are there. Spindler (1974) reported a story from Margaret Read [sic] (1968): A new young teacher was telling a senior chief of the Ngoni of Malawi that education consisted of reading, writing, math, scripture, geography, and drill. The senior chief's response was: "No! No! No! Education is *very* broad, *very* deep. It is not only in books, it is learning how to live" (p. 308). In this sense, children in any school learn not only book knowledge, but also the values that are considered important in the society—the attitudes, behaviors, and world view that will bind them to others in their culture and give shape to their living.

In their roles as secondary socializing agents, teachers transmit values consciously. They exhort children through verbal and visual posters to proper behavior. However, there are other ways in which the teachers transmit values to students through nonverbal signs, signals, and similar behavior. These values are so ingrained that the teacher is not at all aware of what is being imparted. As products of their culture, teachers quite naturally work within the framework of the values of their culture. Competitiveness, independence, scientific and rational knowledge, the importance of the printed word, and acquisitiveness are unconsciously and implicitly, as well as explicitly, encouraged in the everyday activities of many mainstream teachers. The climate of the mainstream classroom reflects the larger society by its approach to teaching and learning: In the United States, there is emphasis, for example, on the task to be accomplished, on linear thinking, on decontextualized information, on "the facts" rather than feelings, on details rather than the whole, on ways of presenting the self to others, on ways of asking questions, and on the attention given to activities. Everything that is done in the school—in the classroom and the corridors, the lunchroom, the gym, the principal's office—is done to direct and ease the transition of the child into the larger society.

In addition to these implicit reflections of the larger society, the school also generates its own culture. Hence, there is a combination of factors that constitute the context of the totality of the classroom. The class structure and climate are influenced by the participants—by the teacher as well as the students. In short, not only do common classroom experiences such as sequential activities, linear thinking, competitiveness, independent work, "Show and Tell," taking turns, and student–teacher relationships reflect the values of the dominant culture, but culturally shaped, unconscious demands of and responses to the needs and fears of the participants further impact the culture into which the cross-cultural students are placed.

Cross-cultural students also face the assumption by their mainstream peers of the importance and need for student participation in ongoing activities as a way of showing competence in the classroom. Among others, Florio (1978) has shown that linguistic or academic competence is not sufficient; knowing how to manage in the classroom (turn taking, sharing, various classroom behaviors) and competence in nonverbal communication are necessary for acceptance. The cross-cultural students must learn not only the language, but also the explicit and implicit rules, assumptions, behaviors, and nonverbal communication—in short, the culture of the classroom and of this new homeland—if they are to make any sense, if they are to experience the congruence they search for. Inherent capabilities and cultural expectations together determine a child's response to the context, as well as the perception of whether the context is affirming and welcoming.

Finally, a brief mention is needed about terminology. A lot of thought has been given to the appropriate term to use when referring to the children participating in this study. *International* was rejected because of the political, not cultural, connotation; *bilingual* was not yet appropriate because the students spoke only their home language. The designations *NEP* (non–English proficient) or *NES* (non-English speaking) were rejected for a number of reasons: They define the students by the standards of the majority culture only; they define the students in a negative term, as something that they are not yet able to do; they define the students in terms of linguistic ability, and this study is looking at acculturation. The students in this study are not yet *bicultural;* that term implies a familiarity with both cultures. Because these students are in the process of becoming, more or less, bicultural, the term *cross-cultural* is used when referring to them, unless the designation of the school system (ESL students) has particular bearing.

Additionally, the term "American" is used by the participants in the popular sense of referring to the United States. However, because "American" technically refers to the entire western hemisphere, I personally have used the term "USAmerican" to narrow the focus to the people of the United States.

AS YOU READ THE STORIES OF THE CHILDREN, THE FOLLOWING PARADIGM MAY BE HELPful as a framework. The results of the study showed that the students did experience some of the phases of the linear adjustment and were on their way to a variety of end-states. Their personalities, self-images, expectations, priorities, and families affected the way in which they were able to handle the challenges of the adjustment. Their presence elicited a response from the host culture. That interaction with the different components of the host culture— with the culture of the school and the classroom, the mainstream teacher, the ESL program, and their peers—resulted in their eventual adjustment or withdrawal. The children were able to achieve congruency with their environment and moved toward a resolution of the challenges; they also felt negative pressures, which forced them

One of the questions that this study does not address is whether the two students who made easier adjustments were able to do so because of cultural similarity (Norwegian and Brazilian) to the host culture. Some research supports cultural similarity for easier adjustment

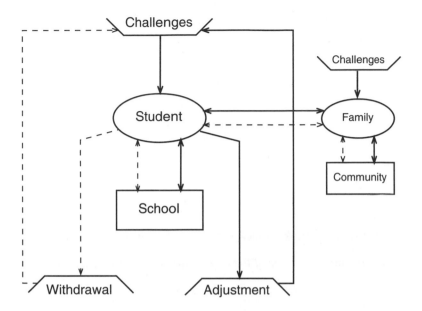

The Process of Acculturation

to withdraw from the receiving culture.[1] For them, it was not an either/or situation, but one in which these positive and negative forces played back and forth in a very dynamic interrelationship. Figure 1 illustrates this process.

> "Where do you come from?" said the Red Queen. "And where are you going? Look up, speak nicely, and don't twiddle your fingers all the time."
>
> Alice attended to all these directions, and explained, as well as she could, that she had lost her way.
>
> "I don't know what you mean by *your way*," said the Queen: "all the ways about here belong to *me* —but why did you come out here at all?" she added in a kinder tone. "Curtsey while you are thinking about what to say. It saves time."
>
> —Lewis Carroll, *Through the Looking Glass*

(Gudykunst and Hammer 1988); other research has found that interactional patterns shaped by the cultures of the children (Brazilian and Korean) was more determinative than cultural similarity (Willett, 1987). Another question not addressed is linguistic similarity, as named by Erik as the reason for his facility with English. This study does not have the scope to address either of those issues.

Winsted

A lush strip of grass 30 feet wide dotted with flowering trees runs down the middle of one of the city's wide boulevards. Further on, an uninviting alley with ramshackle houses opens out to a tree-lined avenue that curves around old, generous, Victorian houses and a lively school. Nearby, a narrow main street bustles with the traffic of eateries and stores. The city of Winsted sprawls over not only many miles but also many neighborhoods, lifestyles, religions, traditions, and ethnicities. This is both the charm and the challenge of Winsted.

The city, in the northeastern United States, was first settled in the mid-seventeenth century, and now the availability of public transportation, well-maintained neighborhoods, high property values, and a nationally known educational system have made this community a very desirable place to live.

The school system and the children in this study are extremely fortunate; socioeconomic class has played a role in this study. However, the challenges faced by the children and teachers in the initial period of acculturation offer insights to those who may find themselves in other settings.

Erik Svensen

This is my last day of observation. Erik has been in this country for three months. His favorite subject is math, and the class had been assigned a math puzzle, a rather complicated system of matching a computational problem on the edge of one puzzle piece with the solution on the edge of another piece. He did not understand the written directions very well and casually asked the only classmate who had finished it how the puzzle was to be put together. She put three pieces together, but did not explain any further. I walked over to see if I could be of help. As we fit a piece here and there, Erik would explode with, "Yes, we found it! Here it is!" The final placement was greeted with two thumbs up and "Great, I did it!" (Observation, December 1992)

Three months before, on the first day that I observed Erik in class, I had had a hard time finding him; I finally identified him by the wispy, light brown, braided pigtail down the nape of his neck—the popular haircut of the year. Nine years old, he had been placed in the fourth grade at the Brush Hill School, even though in his native Norway he would have been in the third. He referred often to his jumping of a grade here, especially when he felt that the homework was very difficult.

Erik's family was in the United States for his father's one year of post-doctoral study at a prestigious university. His father had stayed with a USAmerican family in the United States twenty-five years before, for a year in high school; his mother knew English and his 15-year-old brother, Kristian, had studied it since the fifth grade. Erik would have started English this year in third grade in Norway. Both he and his family said that he had not had any knowledge of English before he came to the United States. According to Erik, the whole family was very happy when the letter arrived inviting his father to come; Erik was eagerly looking forward to the experience.

The Svensens arrived in the United States about one month before school started and, after a brief stay in the large urban center where the university was located, went to visit the father's "American sister" and family. They stayed there a few days while the parents looked for housing. They moved into their two-story duplex in an established, residential neighborhood two weeks before the start of school and spent the rest of the time getting acquainted with the community and locating furnishings for their home. The one problem they saw with their location was the busy street, a main thoroughfare, and the concomitant problems of children playing outside. The parents commented that the boys were very lonesome the first few days because they could not find anyone to play with, in the street or in nearby yards. During this time, Erik was enrolled in the neighborhood school.

Brush Hill School was in the midst of a variegated neighborhood: on one side of the school, large, old, substantial, single-family homes with front porches and lawns, and on the other side, closer to a major interstate highway, homes that were run down, poorly kept, multifamily, and in need of paint and repair. Two blocks from the back door of the school, numerous stores further indicated the urban–suburban mix of this part of Winsted; the physical neighborhood reflected the diversity of the community—economic, ethnic, and religious. There was a comfortable feeling to the mixture as one walked and drove the streets.

Brush Hill School, itself, was a two and a half-story box-like, sturdy, brick building. Walking into the building on a warm, hazy day in September, I was taken aback. This stodgy-looking building exploded into color and space: Recent renovations had made the central office light, accessible, and spacious; bright colors were splashed on corridor walls and contrasting colors on the doorless lockers. Later, as winter settled in, these open lockers could no longer hold all the boots, jackets, hats, mittens, and scarves, in addition to the books, bags, musical instruments, and lunchboxes, so that a riot of colorful clothing spilled out in major disarray all along the corridors. In addition, pictures, paintings, and artifacts from Japan adorned walls, not just in the office but throughout the building.

Approximately 300 students were enrolled at the Brush Hill School that year and about 10 percent of them were in the ESL program, according to the head ESL teacher. In addition to the ESL program, there was a citywide Japanese bilingual program at this school. On the second floor, surrounded by windows on three sides, the bright and airy ESL/bilingual room perched over the street below. A large display, tastefully mounted on the bulletin board, introduced children and adults to the different scripts of the world. Teachers here had an artistic flair, as other bulletin boards were filled with words and images to help the new learners of English and to validate the various heritages represented in the ESL and bilingual population.

Craig DeAngelis had just started as principal at this school. He seemed inundated by the exigencies of a new principalship; however, his spirit was unflagging, and he exuded energy. His approach was that of involvement with the children: He took his turn at bus duty, he sat on the floor with children in the gym for a performance, he wandered around to the classes to get to know them. His guiding philosophy in his role as principal was a multifaceted approach to "help the children." He wanted them to have the requisite skills for the next level, a love of learning that would continue for the rest of their lives, and confidence as learners. Finally, he wanted students to feel worthy, to respect themselves and others. He felt that there needed to be a marriage of the affective and the cognitive.

He noted, however, that since his arrival it had been "an irrational time," because for more than 50 percent of that time there had been a limited job action in force by the teachers. This action had had an impact on his hope to accomplish some schoolwide policies, because faculty meetings were not attended. One of the issues affected was the dissemination of the "Core Values" of the school, a document that was worked on by parents and teachers the previous year, but not implemented as yet. These core values were based on the belief that the children should get similar messages from home and school, and from class to class, about values that are important. These are values "that the students should take with them when they leave this school; that they should absolutely hold on to; that would be quickly identifiable to a stranger coming into the school" (Principal interview, December 7). The draft of the core values included three areas: a strong academic foundation and appreciation for the arts; self-esteem and perseverance; and celebration of diversity and respect for others. How this would take form in the classrooms or at home had yet to be worked out after the end of the limited job action.

From the slice of school life seen for this study, celebration of diversity was already being practiced in different forms: The third-graders always studied a unit on Japan, including interaction with a Japanese artist. Fourth-graders developed this interest further by learning more about Japanese art. Additionally, the fourth grade that was a part of my study, also used a story about Japan for their language arts lessons for a month in the winter, prompting the participating teacher to comment: "Last year a parent told me that her child knew all sorts of things about Japan but didn't even know the national anthem of the United States."

The music teacher taught a Native American dance. It was done with great dignity and appreciation for the heritage of the people. The teacher sensitively and carefully explained the nature of this sedate dance and the occasions on which these types of dances were used in the Native American community. As it was performed by the children in music class, with lights dim and with the rhythmic beat of shakers and drums, one could sense that the children had been moved to be a part of it, as had I.

I also mused that heroes and holidays—some of the tangible aspects of culture—can become quaint oddities in the eyes of the children when presented out of context without an attempt to understand how different cultures, including the majority one, address the same human experience. In addition, being taken out of context also means that often only one dimension is perceived as the whole, with the result that a whole culture and people are reduced to one symbol, which is usually the choice of the majority, not the particular culture. The sensitive presentation of the Native American dance gave a different dimension and an opportunity for the children to experience another approach to the human experience.

A sense of caring for others had not been mentioned as a specific core value, but seemed very palpable throughout the fourteen weeks of the study. It permeated the school and was also reflected by Erik:

> The children in the class are very helpful; the teacher is helpful. Everybody is very nice. They make you feel welcome. (Student interviews, October 5, November 30 combined)

Welcoming, yes, and curious also. I was repeatedly asked, particularly by adults who came into the room, about my purpose. Most were interested; some, particularly those with strong feelings about the topic of acculturation and language learning, shared their feelings. One specialist who came into the classroom during language arts to help two learning disabled children, had the following comment, not about the student who was being observed, but about a bicultural student:

> The reason that Li Bo does not do well and has to come to the Learning Center is because he does not speak English at home. Children cannot gain any fluency if they do not speak English at home.

Later, in the discussion following this statement, she said that her family had come from Russia when she was a child, and their decision had been to speak English at home at all times; it was a trade-off that had to be made. In her opinion, one could not have it both ways.

These are decisions that each family must make; they are not always easy ones, because language symbolizes so much of one's identity. Currently, however, there is much research that shows that a second language is learned better and faster when the first language is maintained at home. Being able to communicate easily is a basic need; frustration against the second language can build up if it is required too soon, particularly in the nurturing environment of the home. Some of the other issues affecting the use of English at home are the level of the parents' linguistic abilities in English; the awkward situation (for the children) of being corrected by a teacher in their imitation of parental discourses; the possibility of having mistakes in English become fossilized through repeated input at home; and the concomitant problems of invalidating a heritage. As Heath (1986) has suggested, the varieties and genres of language a child is exposed to and uses, in whatever language, are important factors for educational achievement, not specific vocabulary.

ALTHOUGH EXCITED ABOUT BEING HERE, ERIK BRIEFLY LONGED FOR THE familiarity of school in Norway:

> School starts at 8:25 in the morning, until 2 in the afternoon. I walk two kilometers to school with my friends. There is recess after every period. The first one in the morning is for five minutes; then the ones after are ten or fifteen minutes. And half an hour after lunch. . . . There is ten minutes to eat and thirty minutes to play outside. (Student interview, October 19)

He also noted some differences between his school in Norway and Brush Hill School:

> There is a large playground there, and there are many recesses and it is quite a lot of fun. Math and swimming are my favorite subjects (Student journal November 10). We swim the whole year long; the whole class has to swim. We get a medal for each thing that we accomplish. My class was pretty smart, but a little noisy. My teacher said I did well in writing and did well in math, but talked a little too much. (Student interview, November 16)

To understand Erik is also to know the sparkle in his eye, the reflection of his feelings in his face, his love of sports. His life in Norway and his life in the United States were crammed with football, soccer, baseball, basketball, and scouts. From two entries from his journal,

> Today I played baseball with some other boys. There were seven boys. After this I played soccer. I think I scored two goals. In gym we also play soccer. (October 20)

When asked about what good thing happened this week,

> I was so happy when I received the scout items [i.e., handbook, badge, necktie, etc.]. (October 29)

The personal stamp of the children was a very important factor in their adjustment. The gregarious children, not surprisingly, made an easier adjustment than the two who were shy. Parents of the gregarious children, when asked what they thought was the major factor in their children's adjustment, replied that it was their social nature. In addition, Erik had the gift and skill of being an athlete, an interest that not only took him out of himself, but also, in U.S. culture, is highly valued. Both gregarious children were also able to take risks socially and linguistically, unintimidated by their lack of understanding the language.

Despite being gregarious and athletic, Erik remembered his first days at the Brush Hill School in this way:

> I almost started to cry the first day of school, only because my mother was not there and I almost did not understand anything. The second day was the same. What I remember was that they had a snack break and I didn't know anything about it, so they shared with me. After that we went out and played soccer and I scored 4 goals. I was happy when I scored all those goals. (Student journal, November 5)

All four cross-cultural children remarked on the embarrassment of not knowing about snacks: It made them feel even more like outsiders. Wanting very much to blend in with the rest of the class was very important to all four students. There were different ways in which each one attempted to become integrated quickly. Some achieved that integration, some did not. While not having a snack can be used as a point of sharing for the rest of the class, for the cross-cultural students it can be another clear reminder of being in unfamiliar territory. It is the type of classroom convention that needs to be communicated in some way to the family ahead of time so that the student does not experience being the center of attention for a negative, rather than a positive, action.

The adjustments to the various classroom conventions the cross-cultural students had to make were probably the easiest because they were the most obvious and concrete. The cross-cultural students all mentioned the absence of regular (i.e., after each lesson) recesses; there were procedures to be learned for getting permission to go to the bathroom, to line up, and to go to lunch. Conventions that required explanation rather than simple observation (e.g., getting one of the students to change a large can of soda at lunch to a more nutritious variety and more appropriate size) took a little longer to understand. Some other conventions that were mentioned by different students were the casual start of school at the beginning of each day, not standing to answer teachers' questions or to recite, and addressing teachers by names (e.g., Mrs. Dinesen) instead of only titles (e.g., Teacher).

ERIK'S MOTHER'S VIEW OF THE FIRST DAY CENTERED NOT ON THE SNACK SHE HAD HAD TO quickly buy, but on separation:

> Erik starts at the Brush Hill School [today]. He is excited about it. First I asked the teacher if she wanted me to stay with him in the class, but she did not want me to. I waited in the cafeteria together with other parents. Erik was crying when I left him. I went back to see him several times, and when he saw me, he started to cry. The teacher said he was fine, but I could see he was not. Maybe he was fine when I was not there? . . . The best thing on the first day was that [though chosen last] he made all the goals of his team in soccer. In the afternoon he seemed like he had forgotten his first school day. When eating dinner, he told a lot of things which the teacher and children had told him. (Parent journal, September 10)

Patty Lane, his teacher, said that she had had a chance to meet Erik the day before school began, before all the children came in. When school started the next day, he seemed very shy and cried when his mom left and again when he found that he did not have a snack. Her assessment of Erik's first day:

> My impression . . . initially was that he kind of looked, tried to look like he was engaged. He'd smile if I caught his eye, and he tried to be there with us, but I know it was hard. (Teacher interview, October 6)

She had presented an activity for the whole class in which Erik was able to participate, much to her surprise, so that by the end of the day, she felt very encouraged. She was therefore unprepared for his reaction the second day:

> He came in and he cried. . . .[H]e put his head down, would not look at me, and I went over to him, tried to talk to him, and tried to tell him to look at me and he wouldn't do it. Finally when he did, I didn't want to embarrass him, because with fourth graders, I know that this is hard. . . . I just was very conscious of how he might be feeling. First of all, not being able to be comfortable with the language and also crying. He was scared, he was upset. So I went in and asked for Susan's help; she is the ESL teacher. . . When he came back he seemed much more relaxed and so that seemed to help. It was encouraging that there was some help there. (Teacher interview, October 6)

Erik's mother added a further perspective to the second day:

> The second day at school was a confusing and frustrating day, too. He
> felt outside, did not understand and could not speak. He cried in the
> morning and did not want to go to school. It was a long day; he is not
> used to being at school until 3 o'clock... The best thing the second day,
> too, was playing. He is not afraid of going into playing, even if he cannot
> speak. (Parent journal, September 11)

A final angle on the second day was the perspective of the ESL teacher whose
help Patty Lane had enlisted:

> I think it was the Friday of that first week [the second day of school], he
> had his head down on his desk in his classroom and he was sobbing. I'm
> sure he just felt completely overwhelmed because he couldn't under-
> stand anything... We have a chart of all the flags of the world and a map
> of the countries [in the ESL room]. So he drew a picture of his flag. And
> he colored it. We were planning to have all the ESL students do that and
> display them... I don't speak Norwegian and I have been able to com-
> municate with him right from the start, in a very elementary way, but I
> could say things to him and he would understand. He could get the gist
> of what I was saying. (ESL teacher interview, October 26)

PATTY LANE'S CLASSROOM WAS A COMBINATION OF VIBRANT, EYE-CATCHING, UNCLUT-
tered bulletin boards and a neat and calm atmosphere. She was solicitous of
her students in many aspects of class; she apologized to the students if things
did not go as planned.

The posters in her room reflected a sense of multiculturalism through
pictures of many children of different races around the words of the song
"The Colors of the Earth" and through the use of the Peters Projection of the
world map. She had been teaching for six years and Erik was her second student who had arrived with no prior English; she had also had other students
with limited English. Patty Lane's class reflected the cultural diversity found
in the rest of the school: In addition to Erik, there were five who were of East
Asian heritage, one of African American, and one of Norwegian; all, except
Erik, were the first generation born in the United States.

During the week after the beginning of school, Erik's mother shared her
thoughts in her journal:

> I talked to his teacher today and was told he seemed much happier. He
> smiled! But he is still frustrated by not understanding anything. And he
> does not understand what his homework is. But soccer is still fun! (Par-
> ent journal, September 14)

[The school f]amily picnic [was] in the afternoon. Erik forgot to eat—
he was busy playing soccer and football with the other kids. (Parent
journal, September 15)

He tried to do some homework—list of spelling words—but it was too difficult for him, so we finally gave up. (Parent journal, September 16,17,18)

THE FIRST DAY I OBSERVED ERIK WAS ON HIS EIGHTH DAY IN SCHOOL. DESKS WERE USU-
ally arranged in groupings. On this day, there were two groups of six desks
and three groups of four. He looked comfortable; he did not look around
nervously; he leaned over to ask a question of a classmate; he exchanged
looks and words playfully with another. The class was math, and the problems had complex language. After the instructions had been given to the
whole class, I wandered over to see how he was doing. The word problems
were very complicated for someone new to the language. Patty was soon
there and showed him pages in the workbook with some numerical compu-
tation that he could do instead. He did the page quickly. Soon, his friend
Ingrid was over helping him with the previous page. She just told him what
to write and he wrote it down. He also understood her when she made com
ments with appropriate actions, such as, "Keep your finger on that." It was a
very playful exchange with her. Shortly after that, Ingrid found that she had
not done the page with a grid on it. Erik was able to help her with that. I also
noted that Erik had already been incorporated into the job assignments.
Since my initial meeting with the teacher, he had moved from "Door Holder"
to "Line Leader."

At snacktime, Patty gave the students the option of eating at their desks
or eating at one of two tables of four or five children. Some children sat at the
table with friends. Erik did not look saddened by sitting alone; although there
was another student at his desk group, there was no interaction between
them. In the middle of the snacktime, he saw someone else in class working
on a project the teacher had set up. He went over and was eating his snack
there when the teacher asked him to go back to his seat until he had finished
eating. The rule was that snacks had to be finished first. He seemed to understand and obeyed happily.

Mrs. Svensen's journal reflects a different angle on Erik for the same day:

Erik was not happy when he came home today. He had no homework for
tomorrow—just reading. I wanted him to do some Norwegian workbooks;
he was not happy about that, but he did a little. He just wanted to watch
TV—and he could not tell me what was wrong. In the evening, however, he
told me that he was bored at school—just sitting there and doing nothing.
(Parent journal, September 22)

ERIK'S EFFORTS TO INTEGRATE QUICKLY INTO CLASS COULD BE SEEN IN SMALL BUT SIG-
nificant ways. For example, when the substitute called the class to "the rug" for
meeting time at 8:45, Erik was there quickly, sitting in the front row of the
circle. He was not disruptive, but a little restless during this fifteen-minute procedure at the beginning of the day. Math was announced and various problems/
projects were assigned. The students were allowed to work in groups at the different projects. Erik approached the substitute with papers in hand; she started
going over the word problems with him. It involved drawing straight lines
through a grid. She spent quite a bit of time trying to explain straight versus
curvy lines, her voice getting louder and louder. Despite the rather complicated
directions of trying to find out how many straight lines could be drawn all starting at point (0,0), he seemed to understand and set off to complete the page.

Just about that time also, his mother wrote in her journal that a Dutch
boy who lived down the street had come over to play with Erik in the afternoon. Mrs. Svensen observed them from another room and noted that Erik

> was not afraid of speaking. He used the words he knew, not afraid of
> making a fool of himself. His older brother was impressed when he
> heard it. (Parent journal, September 25)

Two weeks after the beginning of school, two developments emerged.
One was the amount of peer interaction with and by Erik. On just one day I
noted that he was called over to a window by another boy to see something
outside; he initiated a conversation with the child across the desk from him;
he had at least one child with whom to toss a football back and forth during
recess. The second development was the question posed by Patty Lane to me,
asking whether I had talked with the Svensens recently. Apparently Mrs.
Svensen had been in school the night before and voiced her concern about
how poorly she thought Erik was doing. According to Patty, the parents
seemed to have a lot of restlessness about their child's adjustment.

Their perspective is seen in this journal entry:

> I spoke to Patty Lane after the Curriculum Night. I told her he was frus-
> trated and was bored at school. When speaking to her, it seemed like
> Erik was doing much better at school than he was telling me. Both she
> and [the ESL teacher] said that he understands a lot and tries to speak;
> he is picking up words very quickly. I know that he is an impatient boy
> and wants to know everything at once! They also said that ESL started
> today. Then he would get some homework and spelling words he was
> able to do. (Parent journal, September 24)

The next time I observed Erik, he was not in the room when I arrived for
reading because his ESL class had started. The mainstream class' reading time

was filled with a variety of activities the children were to work on independently as the teacher walked around to help. Erik came in from ESL during the introduction of all the activities. He sat in his seat, and then as the others got up to move around, he did too, until he realized that he was not involved. As the students got to work, Erik got out his ESL workbook. Patty stopped by and reviewed the directions on the first page. He carried on, alone. He went through the pages carefully and correctly, about three of them in fifteen minutes, and came to the end of what the ESL teacher had assigned. After completing those pages, he sat momentarily with nothing to do. Patty, seeing him idle, told him to continue with the rest of the pages. I went over to see if I could help him with the directions.

Mrs. Svensen recorded her son's response to the day:

> Erik came home and told me had got some homework today, and he was very pleased about that. (Parent journal, September 29)

THE ESL PROGRAM IN EACH SCHOOL WAS ANOTHER MAJOR FACTOR IN THE ADJUSTMENT these students experienced. In all four stories of the children there was high praise for the program, from the students as well as the family and the teachers. The students found it a haven; the ESL teachers knew about the students' linguistic problems, understood their plight, and taught material that was understandable. There, the sense of self as a good student could shine; new vocabulary could be practiced and learned; hesitant conversations, initiated. Having much smaller classes than the mainstream teachers, the ESL teachers were able to create a more relaxed yet more focused atmosphere and use more personalized instruction in their lessons.

However, the difficulty of the ESL program's getting started promptly at the beginning of the school year due to administrative procedures also had an impact on the cross-cultural students and the mainstream teachers. Due to the nature of the program trying to fit in to various teachers' schedules, there could be no formal ESL schedule for almost two weeks. Mrs. Svensen articulated here the big difference the regularization of the ESL schedule meant for her child.

> Once ESL started, he was much happier. At once. He got homework and spelling words—words that they had worked on in ESL. He could make easy sentences. I helped him, of course, but I asked the teacher how to do it and he made the sentences. . . So he has work to do.
> [At this point Erik came in to show us the cartoon strips he had made with his spelling words, the same activity assigned to the class for their words, but done with his words.] The mother continued: It is

simple stuff. I didn't help him with this project. He sees the students in class working on the spelling all the time and [big sigh] he can't do it because it is too difficult. So he is very happy to get his own spelling words and then do this too. (Parent interview, October 5)

Erik's first entry in his journal was finally written in early October. It did not mention ESL, but did sum up all his interests of the previous three weeks:

Today I played football. I feel it is a little difficult in school. And I had gym and played football there also. My dictionary helps me a lot. My teacher also helps me a great deal. I think it is very difficult with my homework. I have now made some new friends in school. Their names are Bobby and Wes. I am going to football practice. (Student journal, October 2)

My first interview with Erik came just three days after that entry, two weeks after I had started observing him. Much of the interview was a process of getting acquainted. I asked him what surprised him most about the United States:

Cornflakes. That we don't have in Norway. (Student interview, October 5)

He went on to comment that he liked them and had them regularly during the week. The T/EI informed me that in Norway breakfasts usually are heartier than a bowl of cold cereal.

When asked what he missed most about Norway, he started his answer with a big sigh and then replied what he missed most were his friends and snow. He went so far as to say that probably there was already a lot of snow in his hometown, until he calculated the months and decided that it was still, indeed, fall there also.

In this first interview, he commented that homework was something that he did not understand, especially since he was one grade ahead of where he would have been in Norway. However, his mother helped him. The previous two weeks in class had been very difficult, but he felt that everyone in his class had been very helpful, including his teacher. The length of the school day was also difficult for him.

Approximately three weeks into the school year, I observed Erik with some of the specialists for art, music, library, and gym. Erik's comments about these classes:

Music is easy, gym is easy; art is a little easy and library is not easy because I do not know where the books are located. I am not very excited by art; it is boring. In Norway, art is in the same classroom as other things; but the music teacher is one of the best singers in the area I come

from. Sometimes I like the books I get from the library here and sometimes not. (Student interview, November 16)

The art teacher at Brush Hill School was very careful in giving clear directions. While Erik may have been bored by the content that he was not able to
understand (they were drawing designs found in leaves), he was able to follow
the directions very easily, due to his observations and the teacher's concise directions. In the library, he was in the midst of the students gathered around an
alphabetizing project that the media teacher had given them, contributing to
the general discussion on the order of the letters. At the time when the students
were permitted to browse, Erik went to the nonfiction section and found a
book which he leafed through. He seemed very excited about it and turned to
the child standing next to him to share that enthusiasm. The book itself
seemed much too difficult in language. His mother commented later:

He's not reading the English. He's just looking at the diagrams, the pictures, to see what it is about. Maybe it was the book with the paper air-
planes. It is a book about making things. (Parent interview, October 5)

Physical education class began with stretching exercises. This particular
day, they were to walk, jog, and/or run around the field eleven times to equal
one mile. Erik was one of the first to take off and when he found himself surrounded by four other fellows, he quickly got out of the group and ran faster.
Twice around the field, at a very good pace, tired him out, however, and from
then on, he was jogging and finally walking with a friend.

For chorus they stood on risers and practiced for the Halloween con-
cert. Erik joined right in, at least in hand motions when he didn't know the
words. He had talked about his musical family: His brother and father play
the clarinet; he, the trumpet. When asked, toward the end of the study, to
write in his journal about what had happened in the previous two days and
how he had felt, he noted,

Yesterday we had music and it was quite enjoyable. We sang and raised
our hands and had to think. We had snacks and after that we went out to
play. I usually play soccer. I was glad and attentive. (Student journal,
December 8)

Given the quick adjustment that Erik seemed to be making, I was surprised by Mrs. Svensen's answer to my question of how her own adjustment
was going:

It was not my wish to come here [nervous laugh]. I know I will take care
of the children and have an interest in sewing and I can fill the days with
that. I don't know if it is enough for me for the whole year. But today I

signed up for an English course. . . . I was employed as a part-time occu-
pational therapist this past year. . . . It was not a big job, a few hours. I
live in a small place, and we are two therapists—who shared a job. She
was three-quarter time and I was one-quarter. She is now full time while
we are here and if she likes it, I will have no job when we return. . . . I
have not worked for several years because I liked being at home with the
children. I can always find something to do with all my interests. I am
not bored at home. I think that helps me here not to feel lonely.

JBC: So, in a sense, you were not as excited about coming here as the rest
of the family?

Mrs. Svensen: Yes, not at first. Some things about America are different
from Norway. Especially not feeling safe in the way that I do at home.
You have to look out for the children more here. You cannot send them
out everywhere. You have to look after them. . . . I don't like that feeling.
. . . . And you cannot leave them alone. . . . So, I think that is the most
difficult thing for me to adjust. . . . When we first came, we heard about
the Norwegian student being stabbed in [a neighboring city]. One of the
attackers was a high school student, so it was especially hard for Kristian.
(Parent interview, October 5)

When asked whether the children had expressed homesickness, she replied
that just the previous day they had talked about it. Kristian had said that
there was nothing that he missed. He seemed to be enjoying life in the United
States very much. He particularly enjoyed the freedom to say and do and
dress as he liked. Erik hadn't said too much, but Mrs. Svensen felt that "he
finds it very exciting being here; he is very anxious to learn the American
sports." Mrs. Svensen said that in Norway foreigners are not very welcome,
even nationals who go from one part of the country to another. She felt that
it had been easy to be a foreigner here. As a family, they appreciated the sense
of being welcomed. When asked if Brush Hill School had played a role in that
in any way, she responded,

They told us they were very lucky in having so many children from different countries—an opportunity for them, too. It was nice to hear. We
felt that they were curious about Erik and did not look upon him as an
outsider. They were interested in him. I guess it was a little difficult for
the teacher the first day, so the teacher did not seem as concerned as
she could have, but the situation has changed now. (Parent interview,
October 5)

About a month into the school year, I had the first interview with Patty
Lane. She said more about Erik's first day at school:

I had an activity where they had to talk to the person sitting across from them and find out something amazing about that person or something that that person had done over the summer. I was kind of nervous about that because I wasn't sure that Erik would be able to handle it, but I didn't want to just exclude him and there was no support for him at that time so I tried to be there to help. His partner was wonderful. They came up with a written project by her telling him the actual letters to write down for what she wanted to tell him. And the most surprising thing about the experience was that when I asked them to introduce their friend, he read from his in English beautifully. Now, I was kind of shocked because he seemed to have trouble with her talking too fast, but he read it right from the sheet beautifully.

JBC: Was his partner the other child with Norwegian heritage in your class?

Patty: No. In fact, they have made no connection at all, which I think is interesting. She knows about it, and she has made no attempt to engage, to help in any way. (Teacher interview, October 6)

Patty continued with her thoughts about Erik's adjustment to the class: She felt that math had been going very well during the past month, but that other times of the day were tougher for him since they involved more language.

I know he got, probably, nothing out of [the story read in class]. He was, also, seeing the other kids working and probably feeling like he should be doing something and not just sitting. I guess all this came to a head in a meeting on September 23 or 24 with his mom. She came in and . . . told me that Erik was miserable, absolutely miserable; that he was bored; that he loves to play so she wasn't concerned about that time of the day, but that he was really bored and she was worried about that, under-standably. . . . I told her ESL was just starting in earnest, and I suggested that we meet after he had been through the program a week. We met the following Thursday, and things have disappeared in terms of those kinds of feelings because what the ESL program has provided him with are words he can work on. . . . That has helped him in the classroom, as well. . . . It has made a huge difference. . . . And he is feeling good about that; he is doing homework like the other kids. . . . Things have calmed down considerably and in fact—he's feeling much better because he is doing his own work. When the kids are doing spelling, he's doing spell-ing; different words, but same kind of thing. When the kids are doing math, he's doing math. When the kids are doing reading, he's doing reading in the ESL room. He's in art, music, PE with the rest of the kids. For the most part, I think he's doing well. (Teacher interview, October 6)

When asked if she treated him differently than she did the other children in the class, or had different expectations of him, or changed her teaching style due to his presence, she responded,

> Only in the sense that I don't expect less, but I change what he is expected to do. In terms of homework, he's still expected to do it and he needs to do ten sentences, but the words are different. . . . I find myself talking very slowly, trying to be very clear with him. [From previous experience] I realized that he needs to know the rules just like everyone else. I try not to accept any different behavior than I would expect from the rest of the class. . . . I don't know whether it is a good thing or bad that I haven't changed my teaching style. The one thing I have done is to make sure that after I have given directions to the entire class, I go over to him and try to make sure that in some way I connect with him about what he needs to do. . . . I try to make sure that I get over to him and go over the directions one more time, slowly, clearly, and look at him. . . . I say it could be a bad thing [not changing teaching style] because I don't necessarily change my plan for the day because he can't do it. (Teacher interview, October 6)

When talking about the development of the Erik's English, Patty commented that what she saw first was the development of oral communication. She noted that he now used less body language—holding up a football, for example—and was more verbal. He used the other students' names, which, Patty claimed, he had learned by the third day of school. In light of his performance of reading on the first day of school, she had wondered what would happen with a particular assignment:

> One of the other homework assignments was a current events article to be presented in class. He didn't want to present it. I can understand that. I did not press that issue. With some kids I might have, but I didn't press it because he couldn't present it. He might have been able to read it, but his article happened to be from the local paper about the bilingual program and a Norwegian boy who was in it, and he clearly could not present that to the class. He might have been able to read it, but I'm not sure he could. (Teacher interview, October 6)

TEACHERS' EXPECTATIONS PRESENTED A MAJOR CHALLENGE FOR THE CROSS-CULTURAL students. For the teachers participating in this study, cross-cultural students were held to the same standard of behavior as the rest of the class. There were attainable behavioral expectations, but also some unattainable ones. The immense concentration required in being surrounded by a language one does not understand meant that, particularly at the beginning of the semester, the cross-cultural students would rest and regroup their energies by looking out of the window or putting their heads down on the desks. There was a conflict here, because most of the teachers felt that the cross-cultural students would "just sit and daydream" if not called to concentrate. It was difficult for the teachers to differentiate between energizing and wasteful daydreaming.

Academically, as exemplified here, the teachers changed the specifics of the assignment to meet the needs and abilities of the cross-cultural student. However, expectations that gave the most trouble were those tied to the development of the students' linguistic abilities in English. Teachers seemed to be caught without clear understanding of what skills to expect in what order. At one end of the spectrum were teacher expectations that the students would be able to understand or read or write before they were able to. At the other end of the spectrum were peers in the classroom who were still protecting the cross-cultural students near the end of the semester by telling student teachers, for example, that the cross-cultural students could not understand/read what they were supposed to, long after such protection was beneficial or necessary. It was difficult for the teachers to know how much to expect linguistically from the students. In this particular situation, Erik's outgoing nature and verbal facility made others think that he had more skills than he actually had mastered.

One day, approximately three weeks into the year, Patty started the class a little before 8:45 AM with announcements about school-related issues and class pictures. The announcements had also been written on the board. Interjected into the discussion were corrections by the students of the heading over the schedule for the day: "Friday, October 9" was written instead of the current day and date, Tuesday, October 13. During this discussion, Erik sat at his desk, leaning over it, a little restless. He was not "paying attention with his eyes" as Patty had requested the children to do; he was, however, now and then looking up words in his dictionary.

From that discussion, Patty quickly moved to another by announcing that they had neglected current events far too long. There ensued a discussion about the presidential debate of the night before and about the cities of Cairo and Houston, which had been in the news over the weekend. She asked if the children knew why she might mention those places (two raised their hands), but she did not pursue the topics further in any way.

After current events, it was time for the spelling pretest. While the rest of the class took it, Erik and I went out into the hallway where I read the list made for him by his ESL teacher. After we corrected it, we returned to the classroom, where it was time for math. The students started by correcting the homework as a class, and Erik was soon making a "thumbs up" sign for getting his correct. He briefly raised his hand to answer one of the problems, but was not called on; the lengthy arithmetic equation required for the answer may have inhibited him from raising his hand for a longer or second time.

After math, the children were allowed to get their snacks by desk groupings. Each group was identified by a member's name; Erik's group was identified by his name. Obviously, Erik had become a full-fledged member of the class, with the rights and privileges and many of the responsibilities as well.

Math class on another day, approximately five and a-half weeks into the school year, found him working on arithmetic problems involving the use of the words *hundreds, thousands, millions;* he had no difficulty. Again, as those problems were corrected, he tentatively raised his hand for one answer but was not called on. The response involved understanding, "How many thousands were traded up in the number (320×100)?"

At 10:30, it was time for a snack. Patty decided that on this day they would have snacktime inside and go out after that for recess. Erik ate his apple quickly, put the core in the wastebasket, and returned to his seat to wait for others to finish. Patty and I were at her desk, talking, when all of a sudden Ingrid, who had been bending over the wastebasket eating a juicy piece of fruit, yelled. Erik had gotten up from his seat, walked across the whole classroom, and pinched her bottom. The look on his face was incredulous that he had been discovered—that he had been seen by the adults in the classroom. He was embarrassed; he seemed to know that he had done something wrong. Patty laughed and said nothing. Shortly thereafter, Ingrid went over to chat with him at his desk.

Standing on the playground that day, watching the children at softball, four-square, tag, and soccer, I commented to Patty that Erik seemed to be socially well integrated into the class. Patty said that some teachers felt that he understood much more English than he let on. She wondered about that; she was not so sure. She gave the example of the previous day when they were talking about Christopher Columbus and she asked him to make a sentence using some of the words that were on the board. He became very uncomfortable by the request. She did not press the issue.

This incident made me reflect on an important theory in second language learning for children. There are two different competencies based on the amount of context available to the learner (Cummins, 1981). The ability to carry on an interpersonal conversation with others occurs much sooner than the ability to manipulate academic language. This is a consequence of context-filled (interpersonal) and context-reduced (academic) situations. Social conversations, embedded in context, are easier to manage in terms of vocabulary and structures than is academic language, which uses more formal language to refer to concepts. ESL teachers often hear the comments, "Why does this student still need to go to ESL? We carry on all sorts of conversations." The goal of

ESL programs is to provide the student with language facility in all four skill areas sufficient to the tasks of understanding classwork and textbooks, not just conversation. To be comfortable enough to tackle cognitive/academic language requirements can take up to five or seven years, though second-language learners are rarely in ESL programs for that length of time.

Some observations by Erik's mother also give a sense of his social explorations and linguistic abilities during this time:

> The family we stayed with . . . before we moved to Winsted came for a visit on Saturday. They were surprised that Erik was able to speak so much English after just a few weeks. Seems that he has crossed a border—and he seems much more comfortable by being able to communicate, especially with children. (Parent journal, October 11)

and

> Today Erik went to a Fair with a family we know from the church— alone. They, too, were impressed that his English had improved so much—almost exploded. He seems happy about it too. (Parent journal, October 12)

According to his mother, when she asked Erik if he understood most of what the teacher said in class, he answered: "Not always. Sometimes she comes to my desk and speaks to me, and there are some words I don't understand." The mother urged Erik to tell the teacher when he did not understand her. At this point, her focus shifted to the fact that Erik walked to school but did not play with the boys in the neighborhood, although he had made some attempts. She couldn't figure out if the others were playing but not including Erik or if there was no neighborhood group that played together. That had been one of the hardest things to get used to in the United States.

ERIK'S INCREASING INTEGRATION INTO THE CLASS COULD BE SEEN IN A VARIETY of ways. Six weeks into the school year, at a time when Patty felt that there were a number of unfinished assignments that needed to be completed, she allowed silent reading for those who were caught up on their work and assigned the completion of their various tasks to the others. A peer was called on to give Erik his spelling test; they went happily into the hallway. When they came back, Erik went over to that classmate's desk to look at his new pencil box. Another peer continued to play with Erik's watch even after Patty asked the group to gather on the rug for current events. This time, Erik sat next to Steven, a friend whom he liked and with whom he stood in chorus. They fidgeted back and forth a little, but not disruptively. The current event articles reported by the children dealt with the World Series, Rigoberta Menchu's receiving the Nobel Peace Prize, the support of Bill Clinton by the Kennebunkport Times, and recycling. The first and last presentations elicited considerable discussion between the students and the teacher. The discussion went beyond the presented article on recycling to how to avoid lead in the water. The irony of the Kennebunkport Times' support of Clinton was mentioned. However, while the honor of the Nobel Prize was mentioned, there was no further discussion about that topic. It seemed to me that it was an opportunity missed, as with Cairo and Houston the previous week, to take the children beyond their immediate world, to broaden their horizons. The opportunity to make real the meaning of the posters on the wall slipped by. I reflected that with all the other responsibilities and pressures mainstream teachers have, to also ask them to be aware of any and all opportunities for global consciousness and cultural sensitivity might seem to be a burden; however, not to suggest it is unconscionable in this day.

The following day I observed Erik in ESL class to see if his attitude, behavior, and progress were similar to what was occurring in the mainstream class. At first he was very subdued. Susan (the ESL teacher) said later that that may have been due to the fact that his class was just about to go out to recess when she called him in for ESL. However, he soon warmed up. He and one other student, from France, were the only two in the class. The other student had been having a very difficult adjustment, as indicated by her body language, by the fact that she insisted on speaking French to the ESL teacher and by making comments that had nothing to do with the discussion in progress. Erik, on the other hand, participated well, answered questions, initiated conversation, seemed confident, and was eager to use what English he knew to describe what it was he was trying to say. He was very motivated. When he could not think of a word, he tried explaining it until one of us [Susan or I] caught on to the word he was looking for.

THE OBSERVATION THE NEXT DAY WAS TO HAVE BEEN SCIENCE; WHEN I ARRIVED, the students were out at physical education. After that, for the final half hour of school, Patty had planned a follow-up to the discussion of the previous day on the presidential election. Large stars had been placed on their desks during PE, and they were to write in the stars what would be important to them if they were President. The stars were then to be attached to the bulletin board to complete the background of the flag of the United States, on which pictures and brief biographies of the three candidates were displayed. The children started to write, and Patty went over to Erik to help him. Patty had written on the blackboard: "If I were President, _____ would be important to me." As Patty was talking to Erik about what to write, he looked as if he were going to cry. He looked overwhelmed: He bit his lip, he fidgeted, and his eyes shifted around. She moved away and left him to work on it.

After a short while, I walked over and suggested he tell me what to write and I would write it for him to copy. He seemed a little reluctant. Karen, across the desk, tried to help him recover what he had mumbled to Patty about what he would do—about wild animals. I wrote out what he said about saving them. Then he continued by expressing that saving them was not enough, he wanted to stop killing them. That was added. Then he said that that was not enough either, but that he didn't know how to say what he wanted to. I suggested he try and that perhaps I could help him as I had helped him find the right words in the ESL class the previous day. He did and I did: "If I were President, welcoming people from other countries would be important to me." I wrote out all that he said; he copied it on to the star, added his name and handed it in. He was delighted to see the completed star on the board.

When I had my second interview with Patty the following week, this incident came up in our discussion.

> I think his oral communication is improving in leaps and bounds. He does his spelling and gets all his words right. He is very proud. He comes up to me and says, "I need more words." He seems much more comfortable in general terms with the whole situation here. He is using oral language a lot more. He really will not try written work. I don't know. . .
>
> JBC: You mean written work—like the star?
>
> Patty: Yes, that is a prime example. If I ask him to answer a question by writing it down, he shies from that. And even orally, if I ask him a direct question, it is a blank look first and he says, "Huh?" so I have to repeat the question, and sometimes he can answer me and sometimes not really, almost like he doesn't understand. Then if I ask him to write something like that [star], he . . . first of all he shies away from me, then he doesn't want to do it; he tells me that and at this point I'm wondering the best plan of attack for him because he has come so far. . . . I don't know whether my expectations are off-kilter—because of his oral communication he should be doing more—but we reach a stumbling block when he has to write. (Teacher interview, November 3)

During my second interview with Erik's parents, Erik himself came in and I was able to ask him about the episode with the star. He said that he was upset because he could not write what he wanted to say. Also, he did not un-

derstand what it was he was supposed to do. He finally got the clue by looking at the other children's stars.

An additional order in the general sequence of language acquisition now
falls into place: Receptive skills are mastered before expressive ones. Comprehension of language precedes production; that is, listening precedes speaking,
and reading precedes writing. This is not to say that it is taught in that way,
because students are simultaneously bombarded by information in all four
skill areas. It only means that receptive skills in a cross-cultural student can be
far ahead of expressive skills. Furthermore, because the skills of reading and
writing are generally more context-reduced than listening and speaking, their
acquisition generally takes longer. Language learning is not always a linear pro-
gression, but a cyclic and spiraling one. Nor does language learning necessarily come in regularized, incremental segments, but, as one parent commented,
"in bunches." In the situation discussed here, Erik was able to speak what he
wanted to say, but unable, at that point, to write it down. In addition, speaking
or writing another language is more than simply translating from your own;
there are culturally shaped ways of expression that must also be learned (as can
be seen in some of the translations of the journals).

MY THIRD INTERVIEW WITH ERIK WAS ON THE DAY BEFORE THE NATIONAL ELEC-
tions. On his way to the interview, he was asked by the sixth graders who were
in the hallway staffing the polls to vote for President of the United States. I explained the ballot to him and he was ushered into a little booth where he
could vote. Later, as we were settling down for the interview, I asked him
about his activities of the previous weekend. He proudly stated that he had
bought a cassette player with his own money. Subsequent to this interview, I
wrote the following comment:

> I was interested that when I asked Erik a question, he was very automatic
> in responding to me in English, without waiting for a translation. I had
> to remind him to speak in Norwegian (to facilitate his speaking) to the
> translator. Most of the questions he was able to understand as I asked
> them. (Student interview, November 3)

In this interview, the School Situations Picture Stories (SSPS) pictures
were used as a projective technique. These pictures, used with all four cross-
cultural students, elicited from them some of their interests and feelings
about their experiences. In the first picture, a boy with a nondescript look on
his face is standing next to his teacher's desk. Erik said that the teacher was
correcting the math test while the children were out at recess and that the boy
had gotten a good grade on the math test. The second picture shows three

children with a ball on a playground and a fourth child watching from the sidelines. Erik's story:

> This happened at school. The boy is not allowed to play soccer. The others have said that he is not a good player. Afterwards, the boy asked if he could do the different tests that they have to do in order to play. He was allowed to do them and he did them very well. (Student interview, November 3)

In the third picture, a boy is sitting at a table with books piled on either side; he is staring at the pages open in front of him. Erik said that the boy had had a difficult time with the lessons and that the parents were not home to help him so there was no one to ask. The boy found he couldn't do the homework.

> When the question was asked as to what had happened prior to that particular picture, Erik replied in a lighthearted manner that the boy had thought that the lessons would be easy! (Student interview, November 3)

And what happened after the picture? Erik responded, "The boy went out to play soccer."

It was at this third interview that some time was spent exploring Erik's facility in English. First, it was ascertained, again, that he knew no English when he came to the United States. They spoke Norwegian at home, although his father thought that perhaps they should have spoken English to help the children learn English better. When pushed as to why he thought he learned it so fast, his response was that it was because Norwegian and English were so similar. He gave the example of *kalt* and *cold*. Immediately after this comment, he initiated the fact that he now had four good friends: Wes, Bobby, Steven, and Lars (the Dutch boy). He walked to school with Steven and Bobby.

Even into his fourth interview, two months after the beginning of school, he commented that he still felt that the day was too long. Once again, he compared the length of the school day with that in Norway, where they were in school until 2 PM on Mondays, Wednesdays, and Fridays, and until 11 AM on Tuesdays and Thursdays. The exciting event of the previous two weeks had been the tryouts for the townwide spring soccer team.

At this interview, he was also asked what he liked best about ESL and what he did not like:

> I like best playing [language] games; the worst part is the reading because it is too easy. (Student interview, November 16)

Also at this time, however, he was still experiencing some frustration, as reflected in this journal entry in response to the cue to "tell about something that made you sad this past week":

There was one day when I didn't understand something and I became sad and then I couldn't explain what I didn't understand. (Student journal, November 12)

His mother corroborated the sad feeling he had had in one of her last journal entries:

I don't exactly know how it is for Erik at school right now. I have not spoken to the teacher since the conference in the beginning of October. One day I asked Erik if there still was a lot he didn't understand at school. He answered it was still a lot. But the worst thing was that when he didn't understand, he couldn't explain what he didn't understand. He felt sad about that. (Parent journal, dated only November)

At the next interview with the parents, Erik was in the room and elaborated a little on what he meant by that comment:

One day we had math and we had Mrs. Hosmer [an in-house aide who traveled from class to class to help out at strategic times]. I didn't understand, so I went to her, I said, "What that means?" And she wrote it and read it, and she pointed to it and tried to explain it to me. I didn't understand it. She tried two more times and then went "Phhhhhffffffff. . . . " because she did not know that I am from another country. . . . And this is fourth grade [whereas I would be in third in Norway]. (Parent interview, November 19)

Also at this interview, the parents reported that Erik was now correcting their English pronunciation at home. They had learned "British English and he, American." He did not think they pronounced words correctly.

During this interview, when asked how much responsibility was placed on children in Norway, the mother answered,

Less than here. I think they are more independent here, at home and in school. I have the impression that Mrs. Lane does not want Erik to have too much homework. I asked her to give him homework and I would help him, but I don't think she wanted me to help him much, didn't want to bother me too much. [Sigh] I thought that that is the way it is, that the students do all the work themselves and not bother their parents; they must be more independent.

The father continued:

Maybe she did not want too much stress on Erik. But it was strange, because at that time, we *wanted* Erik to have work to do, because he was so bored. . . . He simply cannot sit down and do nothing; he has to be doing something. . . . Fortunately, we had Norwegian homework he could do. (Parent interview, November 19)

In further discussion, they admitted that if Erik had been able to find friends to play with those first days at school, they would not have felt so strongly about his having English homework. In Norway, children do not have much homework; but here, there was nothing in the early weeks to fill the hours after school for Erik that satisfied either his athletic interest or his wish to become integrated into the class.

When asked what they thought was the biggest factor in Erik's adjustment to the United States, they replied that it was his outgoing personality.

He was on the soccer field the first day, shouting what he thought he was [supposed] to shout to the others. He is an open-minded type. He takes risks, is not afraid of making mistakes. He doesn't like it, but he is able to go on. He is not shy. He loves sports. If he was wondering what others would think of him, he wouldn't join them in playing soccer the first day. (Parent interview, November 19)

PATTY LANE SAW HIS INCREASING ACCULTURATION REFLECTED IN THE INCREASED CONFI-dence and focus that she saw in Erik by the beginning of the third month.

When he is not able to be a part of the group, which he wants to be, obviously, but can't because of the amount of language involved, he will automatically go to his work from ESL; he doesn't have to be prompted to do it; he gets right to it. Before, he used to want to do what we were doing and hoped he could be a part of it. Now, he still wants to be a part of the group, but knows that it is more difficult than he can handle and doesn't wait for me to tell him that he can't take part. . . . He's taking responsibility for what he can do.

He has been listening to the story *Abel's Island*. I expect him to listen and to try to get something from it, though not the whole story. . . . [H]e was part of a group making the island and all the things on it. He loved that. He was an active part of that. Most of the time I expect him to be doing what the other kids are doing . . . and now, [when he is not able to do that], instead of feeling frustrated, he just goes to the work he knows he can do. (Teacher interview, November 24)

Shortly after this, I had the fifth interview with Erik. My comments after that interview read

Most of this interview was conducted in English—it evolved that way. When there was something that Erik did not understand, he knew that he was free to ask the translator; when there was something that I wanted to be sure that he understood, I had her translate. Neither happened too much. His linguistic ability is incredible. (Student interview, November 30)

The same happened with the final interview, during the last week of this study. Activities mentioned during both interviews spoke of numerous visits with USAmerican friends, both alone and with his family. The friends he played with at home were different from the ones with whom he walked to and played with at school, although all attended the same school. His "home" friends lived at a distance, so transportation was necessary.

During the same week, I had gone to observe science; instead, I found a change in the schedule and the children were having math. A timed, number–facts quiz started the period. Erik was one of the first and few to finish. While the students were taking the quiz, Patty told me that the previous day when Susan, the ESL teacher, had come in to get Erik, he had graciously protested, saying that he wanted to stay and work on the Abel's Island project longer—a writing project. He had just started evading ESL, and she felt it showed his comfort level in the classroom. At a convenient stopping place in the project, Erik had gone to ESL. After collecting the math tests, there was just enough time to preview some types of problems that might be assigned for homework. Erik's hand was among many that shot up in answer to the first problem. Although it was not raised as high as the others, Patty saw it and called on him. He went to the board and started to solve the problem. He was progressing correctly when Patty, in her interest to make a point to the rest of the class about what he was doing, said, in a loud voice, "Where'd he get the zero?" Then, a little later and more softly, she added, "He did it right, but where did it come from?" As a student replied, Erik continued solving the problem and could even "validate the answer." He was able to verbalize all of his steps and sat down with commendation from Patty. As the children were packing up their books, Patty wondered aloud to me why Erik's face had dropped during the math problem. She wondered if it had been because she had asked another student about the process he was going through, which she had thought he did not have the language to explain. I suggested that it also might have been that he heard the tone and words of the first part of her question, but not the last.

In the last interview with Patty, she listed Erik's many accomplishments of the previous three weeks: He was to have a change in his time in ESL so that he could be with a group that was doing more difficult work; his reading and comprehension had progressed to a stage where he was beginning to use mainstream-based reading texts instead of ESL-based ones; and perhaps most symbolic of Erik's progress:

Yesterday I happened to forget to give him a separate spelling list. Interestingly enough, he took the spelling test that I gave the whole class, and he really seems to be a perfectionist. He is so diligent and conscientious about his work. He was troubled by the number he had gotten wrong. . . . However, it was a beneficial accident because I now know that he does not need a totally different list. . . . I was really pleased. Also, with this new ESL class, they can incorporate more of the type of thing we are doing in this class. (Teacher interview, December 15)

I asked Patty what she saw as criteria of adjustment.

> I think he has totally adjusted, and I say that because he actively engages in the groups that I set up. . . . He also actively engages with the kids during social times like snack and lunch and recess. He also seems to be adjusted . . . because as he did yesterday, he is not just sitting back and waiting to be handed things. He took control of the situation yesterday and did the spelling [even though it was not his list]. . . .
>
> He was very much distracted at the beginning of the year during group instruction and still sometimes is while we are doing current events, because it is still not something that he is totally comfortable with. That has been the hardest thing. When he can't really participate, he becomes distracted. But he does respect his classmates enough to listen. So, for the most part he is attending to all the lessons, and he is really trying to understand what is going on. (Teacher interview, December 15)

This adjustment that Patty spoke of was reiterated by Erik's mother during the last interview with her. Mrs. Svensen explained that she had asked Erik to write some Christmas cards home to his friends in Norway. He strongly resisted until he came up with the idea of writing them in English. That made it fun. He asked his mother only how to spell a few difficult words and did the rest himself. His mother commented, "It seemed to come naturally." When asked how her own adjustment was proceeding, she said,

> I have found it is easier to get acquainted with people from other countries than Americans, I'm sorry to say. . . . Maybe I'm not too outgoing myself, and I find it difficult just to go to a person and talk to her if there isn't any connection. I talk to people at the soccer field and such, but that is it. It has been easier for me to make friends with people from other countries . . . because we seem to be in the same situation. Maybe they are lonesome here, too, and don't know too many people . . . but all that is at school. At church, it is different. (Parent interview, December 10)

His mother's last journal entry, sometime in November, celebrated Erik's skills and adjustment:

> Soccer is . . . finished. For the winter he is going to play basketball. He is happy about that. It will be a new experience for him. In the spring he is

going to play on a traveling soccer team—or a baseball team—or both, depending on our decision.

In his journal cues, Erik was given a wish list that started out with "I wish that I . . . , that my teacher . . . , that my classmates . . . , that my school . . . , that my family . . ." Here is his:

> I wish that I were a little better in English. I wish my teacher could show a little more understanding. I wish my classmates wouldn't speak so fast. I wish my school could have a larger playground. I wish my family had brought along more clothes. (Student journal, November 17)

Carina Torres

"This land is your land, this land is my land, from California to the New York island . . . ." With the music turned up very loud, Carina was dancing at the table, snapping her fingers and tapping her feet, singing the words, totally immersed in her favorite song. Two groups of ESL students were working at other tables; one student was at the computer, but no one minded the noise. Every now and then Carina would remember to write an answer to a question in the social studies workbook in front of her. She continued to sing as she rewound the tape to start again. She was exuberant. (ESL Observation, October 15)

C arina Torres and her family had arrived in the United States from Brazil on the first of August. They had lived in a downtown hotel for five weeks and were into their second week at a suburban hotel close to the schools the children were attending when I met them for their initial interview. We sat and talked in the hotel lobby on a Saturday morning. They were anxious to move into their rented duplex the following week.

The Torres family was in the United States for a two-year business assignment for Mr. Torres. Mr. Torres spoke English, Mrs. Torres did not. Their son, Riccardo, was in the eighth grade and had studied some English in school in Brazil; Carina, with long brown hair and brown eyes, was 10 years old and in the fifth grade at Valley School. They were happy to be out of Brazil's political and economic woes for a while.

The family was very affectionate and warm and solicitous of each other during the interview. They had questions for me. The parents inquired about additional English lessons for the children as well as for the adults, because they felt that knowing the language was the biggest part of the adjustment ahead. Both children were athletic and the father inquired about the possibilities for town or school soccer teams. The parents had heard about after-school sports in their son's school, but had not yet heard about any in their daughter's school. Also, my role needed clarification; Carina wondered if she did not understand something in class and wrote in her journal about it, whether I would tell the teacher about it. I explained that the journal was for the translator and me alone; however, if the family thought there was some way in which I could help explain a problem to the teacher, I told them I would be happy to do so.

There was a further question about the contents of the journal: Carina wasn't sure what she should write about. When I suggested that it could be about things that happened in school, Mrs. Torres mentioned that Carina, just the previous day, had commented that when the children in class spoke to Carina and she didn't understand, they simply repeated themselves, using the same words over and over, but speaking louder and louder. I indicated to Carina that this was the type of entry that would be helpful.

This reaction that Carina had experienced with her classmates was a common one; when people do not understand what we have said, a first inclination is to think that the listener has not heard clearly and hence we are apt to speak louder and more deliberately, when, actually, the issue is comprehension, not hearing. Cross-cultural students have a difficult time at first, as they get used to the cadence of American English: For example, it takes a little time to equate the distinct, separate words "What did you say?" with the more commonly heard and used, "Whadjewsay?" On the other hand, when speech is slowed down too much, the sense of the sentence gets lost and meaning becomes elusive.

Another response that cross-cultural students face is that when many in the United States hear accented speech, an immediate, first reaction is emotional—that we will not be able to understand what the person is saying, or frustration that the person has not learned unaccented English. Our anxiety diminishes our ability to understand the intelligible but accented interaction; we dismiss the attempt.

CARINA FOUND OUT THAT THE FAMILY WAS COMING TO THE UNITED STATES WHEN HER father came home with the airplane tickets and visas in hand. Having visited

Disney World once, she was most excited about the prospect of meeting new people, seeing new places, and learning a new language; on the other hand, she was very sad to leave the rest of her extended family back in Brazil. When asked what she did not like about the United States, Carina responded,

> There is nothing I don't like. I love everything. I love the city; I loved living in the hotel; I love the school, the parks. What I don't like is not having my family here. . . . If my father came and told me we were going to live here forever, I would be happy; the only thing that would make me happier would be to have the whole family here. I love it here. (Student interview, October 9)

What surprised her the most when she arrived were "the American people." She had been told that USAmerican people did not care for anyone or anything. She was surprised that everyone was so friendly. This feeling was reiterated by her mother at our first interview:

> We had been told that Americans were very unfriendly, hostile, did not care about other people. I have found that to be not true. Our landlady is terrific—she lives in the other half of the house—and has helped us so much. On the first day of school, she came over with a plate of cookies so that the children could have something to eat when they came in [since we hadn't moved yet]. . . . Everything is beautiful in the United States. (Parent interview, October 9)

When asked about her school in Brazil, Carina wrote

> My school in Brazil wasn't too big, but it was a nice place. They taught well and I had lots of friends down there. . . . I was a middle student [academically] because school was a little bit easy. My teacher was very boring. She gave us punishments and threw the eraser at the blackboard and this made a big noise in the classroom. My classroom was a little big. (Student journal, November 10)

In an interview she expanded her description. She had gone to the afternoon session of a private school, which lasted from 1 to 5:30 PM. In grades 1 through 4 there was one teacher for all of the subjects; after that, there was a different teacher for each subject. There was no art or music; physical education was once a week if the teacher happened to be there. She had had some homework, but had not found it hard.

> They weren't too strict at school; though you weren't allowed to put your feet on the desk, and you weren't allowed to [slouch] while sitting at your desk. You couldn't get up whenever you wanted to; each child had

a pencil sharpener, so the only reason to get up was to go to the bathroom. You could do that with permission—but the teacher didn't always
let you. (Student interview, October 22)

Carina thought the system used by her teacher at Valley School—of signing out
in a book when one went to the bathroom—was amusing. She said her father
warned her not to sign out too often, lest points be taken off her report card.

VALLEY SCHOOL, WHERE BOTH CARINA TORRES AND YEVGENY MINDLIN
(another student in this study) were fifth-graders, is tucked away on a corner
lot of a quiet, middle-class neighborhood. It is a two-story brick building,
spilling over its original confines into an addition on the back and a "portable"
on the side. A huge playing field surrounded by trees on two sides borders the
school and the playground next to it where a jungle gym, swings, slide, a basketball hoop, and a paved area provide a large variety of activities for the children during recesses. Inside, the entire building reflected the creativity and enthusiasm of its population, as well as the sense that space was very limited.

There were approximately 500 students in grades K through 6 that year;
an average of twenty-four students per class. In the fifth and sixth grades,
teacher specialization began: There were separate teachers for social studies
and for math and one for language arts and science combined. In addition,
each teacher had a homeroom section. Of the 500 students, 25 percent spoke
a language other than English at home. The multicultural diversity of those
125 students was mirrored in the fact that twenty-two different languages
were represented at Valley School; there was no longer a bilingual program.
Approximately fifty students were in some level of the ESL program.

The office of the principal, Bruce Bunker, was wedged between the
main office and the nurse's room. Although small, it was the nerve center for
the school and was in a strategic place for being aware of all that was happening. Behind Bruce's big desk was a very large window that provided a view of
the front lawn and the street beyond. Posters of Malaysian artifacts and of
children of different ethnicities competed for attention with the set of books
by E.D. Hirsch (*What Your First* [and second, third, . . .] *Grader Needs to
Know*) on his windowsill.

In an effort to understand more about the school, the student profile,
and the underlying attitudes and tenets that shaped the school, I made an
appointment to talk with Bruce. Sitting at a table in his room, he shared a
draft of a document detailing some specifics about Valley School, as well as
one about "Core Values." Due to his early interest and leadership in the area,
the process of arriving at a consensus between the teachers and parents had

occurred before the limited job action had taken effect that autumn. The values that had been decided on were Cooperation, Learning, Respect, and Responsibility. Bruce explained that the appeal of the single words was that teachers and parents could have more leeway in the implementation of the ideas behind the words. He also felt that these single-word core values could be appropriate over the various developmental stages of the children. Plans were made to share this vision with the children in a variety of ways. What had to be put aside during the teachers' limited job action was discussion with the teachers about how these values would be implemented in particular settings in school.

As principal, responsible for the atmosphere of the school, Bruce felt that the core values would channel his approach. The values represented what the children needed in order to be prepared for the rest of their lives. High test scores were not mentioned by the parents, although academic rigor was; both parents and teachers agreed on this issue. In fact, in the coming year, a new math program was to be instituted wherein concepts were taught at a much earlier age than usual.

When asked about the impact of the bicultural and cross-cultural families on Valley School, he replied that they had had a great impact. The previous year, there had been a special booklet printed for the annual International Night. The booklet was a compilation of thirty-four general questions submitted by children and answered by nationals of all ages from fourteen different countries.

Despite this enthusiasm, throughout the three months of the study I felt a pervasive tension symbolized by the multicultural posters and unicultural books in his office. It seemed to me that a tension between openness and resistance—an ambivalence—floated in the background throughout the study. I was curious whether anyone else felt it or would mention it.

CARINA'S FIRST DAY AT VALLEY SCHOOL DID NOT SEEM TO HAVE BEEN VERY traumatic, according to her teachers. Asked at their first interview to share their impressions of her first day and subsequent adjustment, the answers dealt more with the subsequent adjustment than the first day. The social studies teacher responded that Carina was no longer in his class because the work that he was doing was too difficult linguistically for her; she was in ESL for that period. Surprised by this arrangement, the science/homeroom teacher talked about Carina's social nature, and the math teacher talked about the difficulty in getting homework back from her. Pushed one more time about the first day, they responded that she had acted age-appropriately. Carina herself had this to say in her journal:

On my first day of school I was a little bit nervous and I felt that if someone asked me something I wouldn't understand anything. And I had to answer some questions in the classroom about myself but I didn't understand anything that was written there, so one girl came to me and explained to me some things, then I understood better. At recess I looked for her and we got together and I asked her her name. She answered, "My name is Mary." . . . She has been my friend since the first day. (Student journal, November 5)

When asked how long it took for her to feel comfortable in the school, Carina answered,

[A]bout three or four days because everyone helped me and was so nice to me. Everyone plays with me, is patient with me, is friendly. (Student interview, October 9)

Her mother remembers that Carina was very scared on the first day of school: "She acted like a two-year old." By the time of Mrs. Torres' first interview, when she shared this, Carina was "playing with everyone and approaching everything with curiosity." Asked what made the difference, the mother responded,

[H]aving a secure base of operation, that is, a home instead of hotels. Being able to grab a bite to eat when she wants, to play with friends, to go out to play meant a great deal in the adjustment. Also, she continued to find out that Americans are not unfriendly; she had been very cautious about that. (Parent interview, October 9)

ONE OF THE THINGS THAT CARINA LIKED ABOUT SCHOOL IN THE UNITED STATES WAS the arrangement of desks. "Everybody sitting together in groups is much better because people can be near each other," she commented (Student interview, October 9). In Brazil, desks were in rows.

The informality of the classroom was a theme that kept cropping up in the interviews with the children. Coming from cultures where desks were in rows, students stood up to recite, oral examinations occurred frequently, and the teacher was seen as inaccessible, they were surprised about the more informal atmosphere in their schools and classrooms in Winsted. The informality of the classroom and the flexibility of the daily schedule diminishes structure in general from the students' schoolday lives; with no rigid, clear-cut rules to follow (e.g., standing up to recite, oral examinations), it is more difficult for cross-cultural students to gain a basic understanding of how the class operates. Furthermore, children coming from formal classrooms can be bewildered by the different relationship between student and teacher, by the centrality of the student (vis-a-vis the teacher), and by the few formal guidelines for behavior in U.S. classrooms (even, for example, the teacher sitting on the floor or having a cup of coffee during class). Some cross-cultural students might interpret the atmosphere as a lack of respect and may resist in order to maintain what they deem a proper demonstration of respect for the teacher and for education in general; others may interpret the atmosphere as devoid of all control and act inappropriately instead. Change in the classroom culture is a challenge to which cross-cultural students must adjust. Carina's mother summed up the centrality of the student in the United States vis-a-vis the importance of the larger community (parents, teachers) in Brazil:

> Here the most important things in school are the children. In Brazil, not; the school and the teachers are the most important; then come the children. (Parent interview, November 4)

Her comment also reflects the differences between the two cultures on the importance of the individual or the community (family or larger). Students and their families who come from cultures where the larger community is more important than the individual find this new emphasis a challenge. Alternatively, mainstream teachers are impacted when the family makes a decision that prioritizes family need over the student's individual need.

Due to this sense of community and her outgoing personality, Carina loved the frequent rearrangement of desks; she got to meet more people that way. In both Sheila Dinesen's and Donna Devereaux's classrooms, desks were arranged in groups of four. Sheila Dinesen was the homeroom and science teacher for Carina, and she changed the class seating arrangement more than once a month into many different configurations of desks and students. Donna Devereaux was the students' math teacher; in her room, the children sat in a different place each day. As they entered the classroom, they picked a number from a box held by Donna and sat at the desk that had a matching number. When asked why she mixed students up in this way, Donna replied that it gave "the children an opportunity to work with all different kinds of people at all levels of ability."

MY FIRST DAY OF OBSERVATION WAS ON A MONDAY, EIGHT DAYS INTO THE school year. Math was on the schedule for the hour I was there. When I walked in, Carina saw me; her eyes sparkled and she smiled at me. Donna Devereaux's room is large and airy, with windows along one side and bulletin boards on two walls depicting neatly arranged displays of math concepts, facts, "problem of the week," and steps in problem solving. During peer correction of the homework problems, Carina had paper in front of her, but Lara, sitting next to her, did not. The answers they were correcting were numbers, and Carina was mouthing the words as the teacher said them. She kept close contact visually with the teacher at all times. After this, the teacher directed the students to open their books to the concept under study; Carina continued the visual contact with the teacher and the overhead projector she was using. She did not look at her book, which most students were doing. The new homework assignment came next, and Carina wrote in a small notebook the assignment that was written on the board. An additional page of problems had been handed out, which the students were allowed to work on for seven minutes, until the end of class. Everyone got to work quickly. Donna Devereaux walked around during this time to look at everyone's work. She asked Carina for her homework; Carina did not understand what it was she was to give her. Lara (a Russian immigrant of three years) tried to explain to her what the teacher wanted, but Carina continued to look confused. There was a very brief exchange between the girls. Finally, Lara explained to Mrs. Devereaux that Carina had had ESL homework the night before and so had not done the math homework. That was not acceptable to Mrs. Devereaux who insisted that math homework needed to be done along with the ESL homework each night. Carina took out her notebook and wrote something down.

Ramifications of this incident became clearer at a much later interview with Carina. At the end of the interview, I asked her if there was anything else she wanted to share. She said,

> One thing that is very different here is the amount of responsibility that is placed on a student. In Brazil, the teacher was always on your back about remembering to bring in your homework or do what needs to be done. Here, the teachers expect you to do it without reminders. Here, you have to show the teachers that you are responsible; in Brazil, you don't have to do that. (Student interview, October 22)

CARINA WAS ARTICULATING ONE FACET OF ANOTHER CHALLENGE FACED BY CROSS-cultural students: the image of the student. The importance of the individual in U.S. culture is reflected in ways apparent and assumed in the classroom culture. Carina had noticed the teachers' underlying attitude toward all students: Students were to be responsible for their work. There was a sense in which students in the United States fashioned their own identity; this is also borne out by a study by Staton (1990). For Carina, identity had been prescribed by the community. The implication for the cross-cultural students is the emphasis in U.S. classrooms on internal direction and control, not external; students seem to have more control over their fates. The students are responsible, for example, for getting their work done, for going from one step to the next in a project, for making arrangements for makeup work. "Responsibility" was one of the core values of the school; for Carina it was a quick awakening to a more independent perspective; it was also a shift from communal responsibility to individual responsibility. This fostering and expectation of internal control surprised Carina, who was accustomed to more external control—her parents and her teacher telling her what she could or should be doing.

Mrs. Torres' perspective on the amount of responsibility given to children was that it was greater here than in Brazil.

> Here they are responsible for their own things. In Brazil, the parents do everything for the child. The parents are like mother hens. In Brazil, if the father doesn't want the child to do something, he will say, "You are not going to do this because I don't want you to," but here, the children decide what they want to do, what they don't want to do, what they want and don't want. (Parent interview, November 4)

This value of individual responsibility also spilled over to the home, unfortunately in Carina's eyes. During the sixth week of school, in an interview with Carina, I asked,

> Last time we were here, you made a good point about the amount of responsibility that children in the United States have, more than in Brazil. How is that going?
>
> Carina: It is bad because my mother called a friend in Brazil and told about this here and now that mother makes her child work to buy her lunch at school. . . . Now I have to do the car and the yard, even though I didn't have to in Brazil. (Student interview, November 19)

Another facet of the emphasis on individualism in a classroom is reflected in the choices students were presented in class. This was another implicit assumption of the culture of the classroom. Students could choose how to proceed with their projects; they could read whatever books they wanted to for silent reading; they could write reports of their own choosing. Choice was much more prevalent than in the classrooms the cross-cultural students had come from. The importance of the individual and her or his decisions became clear. Asked if it was difficult for Carina to be presented with so many choices and decisions, her mother responded that Carina did not have the necessary experience to make wise choices. She had never had to choose in Brazil.

IN ADDITION TO THESE DIFFERENCES IN THE IMAGE OF THE STUDENT, THERE WAS also a disparity between what these cross-cultural students considered to be appropriate behavior for "good students" and the behavior of their peers in the classroom. Allowing feet on the desks (which all four cross-cultural students mentioned), long earrings and fingernails, disregard for the authority of the teacher (as evidenced by students correcting the teacher) were not indicators of "good students" in the minds of the cross-cultural students. When the cross-cultural students acted out of their *own* cultural understandings of how "good" students should behave (e.g., serious, studious, a little aloof), they were sometimes misunderstood by peers and teachers.

WHEN I ARRIVED AT 8:30 AM ON A RAINY DAY, CARINA WAS SITTING AT HER DESK, quietly listening to the teacher explaining something to a small group nearby. Carina smiled at me and continued looking at the teacher. At 8:45 there was a brief lecture on class procedures regarding homework and snacktime. Through it all, Carina watched Sheila. The class was then instructed to move to the Author's Corner. As the students shared their book reports with their teacher and classmates, Sheila kept urging them to "use your own words; change the author's words and say it your own way." By the time I left, Carina was cradling her head in her arms. Being surrounded by a foreign language all day is an assault on the senses; trying to make sense of it, especially through only one channel (auditory), is very difficult; particularly early in the experience, it is enervating and exhausting. Listening takes energy, and it was necessary for Carina to recharge herself with a break.

While listening and trying to make sense of what was expected was mentally tiring, physical exertion of athletics was welcome. During the second week of school, I observed Carina and Yevgeny in physical education class. It was evident that Carina enjoyed sports very much. When I arrived at the gym, the teacher was just finishing the instructions for a game that was to follow. The directions sounded complicated: "terminators and terminator assistants; blue teams, yellow teams, and red teams." At the end of each round, those who "had survived the attack" were counted. The teacher would call for all members of a team who "had not been eliminated by the terminator to raise their hands." Terminators were chosen by the order in which they had been picked to be on a particular team. Carina was never a terminator, though she was very much involved in the game, darting in and out, helping her team. I asked the teacher how the ESL students could understand what was going on. He replied that there was a girl who knew Russian to translate for "the boy." When I asked who translated into Portuguese, he seemed surprised and said, "Oh, the one with the long, brown hair? She catches on. They both know they can come to me if they have questions. It is a pretty universal thing that when you are hit by a ball, you are out, so they try to steer clear of the ball."

Carina's athleticism and outgoing personality enabled her to blend in with the rest of the fifth graders. Ignoring the complicated language, she watched and quickly caught on. Her personal attributes again helped pave the way for her adjustment.

In addition to physical education, in the course of the fourteen weeks, I observed Carina in music, art, and library. One library period was literature-based and another was skill-based. In the literature-based one, Carina was not able to follow along the stories that had been chosen for the fifth-graders for the week before Halloween. In the skill-based period, at the beginning of the twelfth week of school, Carina and her partner were to find information in certain periodicals and then report to the class what they had found. At the time for the whole-class discussion during that period, Carina jumped right in to read some of the answers she and her partner had written. After this exercise, the students were allowed to search for books "to read to your first-grade partners."

Back in the classroom, I inquired of Sheila about that program of reading to first-grade partners, so that I might see how the cross-cultural students did with such an event. She explained that there were twenty-five fifth-graders and eighteen first-graders. This activity occurred during language arts, so Carina and Yevgeny would not participate because they would be in ESL. When I commented that they had already picked out the books to read, she replied that she was afraid that if they participated this time, they were going to want to participate in the activity all of the time.

It was a terrible shame that the cross-cultural students did not participate in this cross-grade activity; it would have been a terrific boost to their morale. Because the ESL schedule can be flexible, particularly for such important occasions, this was truly a missed opportunity for both the cross-cultural student and the first-grader. For so much of the day cross-cultural students are in the position of receiving help; for them to feel that they can be of help to someone else is a great confidence-booster. In addition, their participation could have worked out as a rich experience for the first-graders to understand the process of learning another language.

IN ART, CARINA ENJOYED THE SOCIABILITY OF THE CLASS. IN THE MIDDLE OF A crowded table of ten students, she had to be reminded to listen to the teacher's explanations. In music, also, Carina's assigned seat was in the midst of her friends. They did not talk much, but shared the music. She participated as best she could in the singing, although she did not answer any of the questions asked by the teacher that involved listening and following notes.

I asked her about all of these classes, what was easy and what was hard. She answered,

> Gym is easy. I don't understand the teacher, but I look at the children and do what they are doing. Library is not. Art is easy, music is easy. . . . They are easy because I can see the people doing things. And they are fun. In the library, I can't [watch others for clues]. (Student interview, November 19)

Writing in her journal about something that was confusing or strange to her, she had said,

> Art—when we cut out something that looked like a fish, the teacher said it was a little OK. When we cut out something crazy, the teacher thought it was wonderful. (Student journal, December 2)

DURING THE THIRD WEEK OF SCHOOL, I ARRIVED AT SNACKTIME. CARINA SAW ME ENTER and came over and offered me a caramel. I asked her about her new home, which her family had just been able to move into the previous week. She indicated that she liked having a room of her own away from her brother, that she had friends in the neighborhood. When asked if they were classmates, she said no, not class, but schoolmates. She offered me her new telephone number.

Science came next and the students began analyzing the life in the pond water they had collected the previous week. There were certain procedures listed by Sheila that each child was to perform and, on completion, check off. Some of the procedures needed to be verified by a classmate or a teacher. There were approximately twenty-two of these procedures; Mrs. Dinesen had selected eight that she felt the cross-cultural students could do with their limited English. Students were gathered around tables, splashing water out of their containers as they tried to find, chase, and catch the various creatures in the water. Carina was interacting with others at the table with "Oh, look at this!" a couple of times; at another point in the period, her friend Mary said to her, "I'm going to get you something," and went off to find a vial of a chemical solution that was being passed around to make the shrimp move a little more slowly. Despite not knowing too much English, Carina was able and willing to use what she did know; which, in turn, enabled her to interact with her classroom peers. This interaction smoothed the way for more friendships. Emphasis on verbal communication is another priority in U.S. culture and another implicit assumption of the classroom culture; often, if a student is consistently shy or silent in class, he will have a hard time making friends or she is thought to be less than intelligent.

At the end of the first month of school, I interviewed Carina's mother in the duplex they had recently moved into. The Torres' home was on a narrow, hilly street that is largely residential. They shared the front entry as well as the good-sized back yard and large driveway with the owner of the house. The two families had become fast friends already; the doors on either side of the entry way were open most of the time, and children from both families went back and forth freely.

At this interview, Mrs. Torres greeted us at the door with an apology that she had not had time to write in the journal because she had been too busy getting the house and children settled as well as getting acquainted with the neighborhood. She was delighted with the United States; life was much easier here than in Brazil.

> There is more time to be a housewife, since there are such things as school buses; keeping the house clean is much easier because there is not the pollution problem that there is in Brazil.
>
> Where we lived in Brazil [northern city] was difficult, but we had good friends, which made it easier. Northern Brazil does not have the [amenities] of Rio, where we used to live, but having friends makes it a good place to live.
>
> Here we have two good friends from Brazil who have been here for three years. We all get together about once a month for dinner at [the suburban motel where they had stayed]. (Parent interview, October 9)

When asked about the stories that Carina brought home from school, Mrs. Torres said that most of the stories were very positive. There had been only one incident in which Carina was unable to explain to the teacher a problem with a boy who accused her wrongly. Carina loved the animals that were in the classroom. Mrs. Torres thought the principal was wonderful; she was impressed that he had been at the bus stop on the first day of school to talk with parents and children. She continued with her assessment that Carina had had problems at first with homework, but that after Mr. Torres had consulted with the teacher, the issue had been resolved: The science teacher seemed to be have been waiting for Carina to learn some English before expecting her to complete the homework; the math teacher had not thought waiting was necessary. Carina had been confused and had not understood which homework she was to do and which she was excused from.

Mrs. Torres compared Valley School with the junior high her son attended; the latter seemed so much better. When asked why that was, Mrs. Torres answered,

> They are able to pay more attention to the students there and there is time after school to stay at school and figure out the homework. (Parent interview, October 9)

She expressed this feeling at the end of the interview:

> This experience is good for my husband; it is a job promotion. But it is really best for the children because of the exposure to another culture and the good education they are getting. (Parental interview, October 9)

Unfortunately, Carina's teachers did not feel positively about the quality of Carina's input into that education. At the first interview, their perspective on Carina's homework came up. Donna Devereaux commented,

> She . . . does very little homework. I've written it down, talked to her father, but there doesn't seem to be any follow-through there. Math is something concrete. You don't need language for numbers. She is really doing nothing. (Teacher interview, October 14)

The other teachers agreed on Carina's lack of effort and commented on her social nature. Sheila said,

> I've seen my girls, one in particular, throw her arms around Carina and say, "Come on, let's go out and throw the ball today, shall we?" babbling a mile a minute, because that is her personality. Carina doesn't have a clue about what she is saying, but she smiles.
>
> Donna: She has a beautiful smile, she really does. (Teacher interview, October 14)

At the end of the interview, I posed a question concerning the relative importance of social and academic adjustments. Donna responded to that question:

> Carina will come along socially, but I am very concerned about her academics because I don't feel that this kid is highly motivated, and that bothers me because unless she becomes highly motivated, she is going to fall behind. . . . I write down everyday in her notebook her math assignments, and I am not getting any back. So there is no parental follow-through. . . . She is not doing fifth grade work right now; she's not doing any work for me. (Teacher interview, October 14)

Sheila and Donna continued talking as they picked up their lunch dishes:

> Sheila: Does she call you Mrs. Devereaux yet?
>
> Donna: No, "Teacher." She doesn't call me much of anything.

JBC: That is a term of honor, you know.

Sheila and Donna: Ohhh?!

Teachers in the United States are accustomed to being called by their names, indeed, by their last names preceded by a title (e.g., Ms., Mr., Mrs.). It is another facet of individualism, a sense of our own identity, that makes this important. In many other parts of the world, honor is bestowed by calling the person by a title; the individual does not have the importance as much as the larger community. For example, in Turkey a child's relatives, on either side of the family, have totally different titles and are called solely by those titles, a custom that applies to most of the extended family. People are known and described by their relationships. When differentiations need to be made, they are often made using a title with a first name. Instead of assigning her teachers into group anonymity (as is perceived here), Carina was showing respect for the person and the profession.

FOR CARINA, LIFE IN SCHOOL CONTINUED TO BE VERY POSITIVE. SYMBOLIC OF her eager participation in class, Carina's hand was up frequently when Sheila asked weekly for volunteers to do the classroom jobs, such as taking care of the animals, running messages to the office and to teachers, and watering the plants. Carina's favorite job was feeding the animals. She did it often. Asked about how academic work was going, she responded with how much better she liked schools here than in Brazil. She especially liked science, which has a much more "hands-on" style; she particularly liked field trips and working with the microscope. In Brazil, it was only book knowledge.

> It is easier [here] because in Brazil we have to memorize. . . . Doing it this way [as in the United States], you don't memorize, you learn and it never leaves you. In Brazil we "eat a book" because we have to memorize the whole thing. (Student interview, November 19)

In math, the teacher gave clearer explanations than in Brazil and played games with the students. Carina enjoyed doing math homework here. She admitted that there had been a time when it had been hard to do; her mother did not speak English, so she had had to wait for her father to help her. Her father had not gotten home until 7 PM and had had to shower and eat dinner before he could help her with the English section of her homework. However, that situation had improved.

For those students coming from cultures where learning is primarily through emulation of the authority (whether book or teacher), cooperative learning, or working in a group, or learning from peers, or learning from one's own discovery and construction of knowledge are all new approaches. Because teachers are unconsciously apt to assume that their students learn the same way they do, being sensitive to the varieties of learning styles, particularly of students brought up in other cultures, is very important. Learning styles are influenced by culture in the socialization process within the family and community and by ecological adaptations, and as such, are somewhat a reflection of the larger culture. Therefore, students coming from other cultures who have not been socialized into the dominant culture may bring a different set of tendencies or sets of patterns to the learning experience. Learning styles of students can vary over the extent to which they are oriented to immediate surroundings (field-sensitive) or not (field-independent), the amount of structure they are accustomed to, and their different modality preferences (Bennett, 1995). One or another learning style is not better; there is no value judgment involved. It is simply a fact of difference. A continuous clash of styles between teacher and student can mean frustration for both. Identification, recognition, and understanding of the difference can help both cross-cultural student and teacher.

AT THE START OF THE SECOND INTERVIEW WITH THE TEACHERS, ABOUT SIX weeks into the school year, I asked about the previous two weeks. Sheila spoke of Carina's increased interest in doing a written project that had not been one of the eight procedures that she had expected from the cross-cultural students: Carina had wanted to write up her observations. "She became very motivated yesterday," was the way Sheila saw it. When I asked if that meant that Carina was doing more than was expected, Sheila said,

> Oh, I wouldn't say more than I am expecting, but more than she was. . . .
> She is not killing herself to do these procedures, but she is making more
> of an effort than she was. It is all relative. It is not more than I expect. It
> is something that I think she might be able to do. (Teacher interview,
> October 28)

Some time later, Sheila was pleased to tell me that Carina had done a very good job on the write-up of her observations.

Continuing in the interview, when asked about the math homework, Donna replied that Carina was doing more, "She is coming along."

> When we have word problems, I try to tell them they don't have to do it.
> From what I can gather, her father is not home a lot to help her. So it really has to be something she can look at and more or less get it on her
> own. I try to give her the computational stuff. She is doing that. (Teacher
> interview, October 28)

An interchange between the teachers about the differences between Yevgeny's and Carina's facility in English brought up the question of previous knowledge of English. According to Carina's registration form, next to "years of English" there was a dash, indicating "none." In the next interview with Carina, during the eighth week of school, I asked her about it. She said that she had had a little English instruction in her school before she came to the United States. Asked if that was why she seemed to be learning it so quickly, she responded,

> My father told me that even if I don't know a word in English, I should try to explain to the person what I want to say, and that person will help me find the word. So that is what I do. (Student interview, November 4)

During one observation in ESL class, Carina was helping Yevgeny on the computer. She knew the procedure and was happy to show him. She also wanted to show me her compositions. I picked up her composition about the Mayflower, and Yevgeny immediately put his copy into my hand as well. At the end of the period, they did not want to leave. The feeling in the room was one of a refuge: The children were comfortable, they were able to accomplish assignments and were proud of their work, and they did not compare unfavorably with peers—they were with peers who were having similar difficulties. Carina's affect in ESL was similar to that in the mainstream classroom, although a bit more expressive, as evidenced by her delight described in the epigraph at the beginning of this chapter.

During my interview with Carina's ESL teacher, she commented about Carina's knack for picking up on the pragmatics of the language, that is, on knowing what is expected and wanted in a conversational interaction. Her knowledge of English was not an academic, learned one, but a social one. Again, it was her *use* of the language, not particularly her knowledge of the vocabulary, that was important.

Asked in the third interview how she felt about her progress in English, Carina replied that she thought it was "pretty good":

> My father said that the most difficult thing was to talk at the gas station and on the telephone. And you told me that I was pretty good on the telephone [referring to a conversation she and I had had when trying to set up an interview date with her mother]. (Student interview, November 4)

When asked how it was that she was able to talk to the other children so much more than Yevgeny, she said,

> Because he is very shy. Sometimes I have to pull him to play. On the playground, he just stands and looks and never asks if he can play or not. He wants to play, and he has more friends here from his country than I

do. He wants to stay with those friends all the time. Sometimes I talk to the girl in the other class in Portuguese, but usually I play with my friends. (Student interview, November 4)

It is interesting to note that Carina differentiated a compatriot from "her friends." Time and again that was true for these students. Three of the four students had compatriots in their classes. One was used as a translator by the teacher, but there did not seem to be much friendship between the student and the compatriot. In the other two situations, no connection was made. A common language or a common heritage does not necessarily mean a common friendship. Neither was there an automatic relationship simply because two or more went to ESL class together. A friendship may occur because of an understanding of the experience, but there is not an "ESL language" in common.

A comment I wrote at the end of this interview with Carina remarked on her rapid progress in English. At almost two months into the school year, she had been able to understand most of the questions in English, but had used Portuguese for ease of expression in most answers.

When asked why she thought Carina was learning the language so quickly, Mrs. Torres replied that it was, first, the ESL class. Even though the school might not be as good as Riccardo's, still it was teaching Carina English. Second, Carina was always out playing and talking with people in the neighborhood. Third, they hoped that Carina would soon be in sports and in that way meet more people and make more friends. Mrs. Torres' perception about her daughter's attitude toward making mistakes or taking risks was that if such a situation happened again, she would do better the next time. Carina didn't seem to get embarrassed at all. Both Carina and Erik Svensen were gregarious children who sought out others easily, whether on the playground or in the classroom. This gift to be able to get outside of themselves and their own insecurities played a major role not only in learning a language, but also in making friends and in how they were perceived by their peers.

Carina's responses to the SSPS pictures reflected more thoughts and feelings about her experiences. The first picture showed a girl standing next to the teacher's desk:

> The girl looked sad, looked like she had done something wrong on the test. It was a science test. The teacher had explained the information, but the student hadn't paid attention to the teacher. So then, on the test, she did something wrong. In Brazil, if you do something wrong on a test, you stay after class; that is your punishment. She has to correct it. Or it could be that she will take the test again.

The second picture was the playground scene:

Some children are playing soccer, and the child asked if she could play, and they said "No." Why? Because they only want three to play, not four. There had been five children playing, and it hadn't been good. She is wondering why she can't play. It was the other kids' fault [when there were so many], so why not let me in? The kid will play with other children, not these.

The third picture was of homework:

The kid is studying and does not want to do any more. She has been studying a lot; she has finished the other two books. She does not understand what is in front of her. She is thinking about going out and playing. She's going to go and play soccer.

The fourth picture was of a father and mother and child standing in front of a desk that has the sign "Principal" on it. Carina's thoughts:

She did something wrong, and the parents had to go to talk to the principal. The girl did not do well on her test, and so the parents had to come to talk to the principal. She is thinking about her punishment; she will be [grounded], and she will be spanked. . . . This happened before school. She will go to class all day and then when she goes home, she will get punished. . . . She is anxious and is thinking that she will never do that again. (Student interview, November 4)

In addition to the SSPS pictures, two books were used as projective techniques with all four children. These books, *Angel Child, Dragon Child* by Surat and *I Hate English* by Levine, describe experiences of children who also were newcomers to the United States. The books provided windows onto the affective as well as cognitive landscapes over which the cross-cultural children had traveled.

In discussing each book, when asked what she thought about the book, Carina's first impulse was to give a verbatim of the story line. The T/EI felt that Carina had not had much experience in talking about a story other than to answer questions about the events and details in the book. That was the way to show that she remembered what she had read. The concepts of analysis or synthesis of stories were unfamiliar to her.

At the parent interview on the same day, Mrs. Torres said the month since our last interview had been very difficult. She and her husband had gone twice to the school to talk with the teachers. The teachers seemed to think that Carina was doing fine, but the parents disagreed. Carina wanted only to play; she said she had no homework. When her father tried to explain things to her, Carina would tell him that he was wrong. They felt that she pretended that she did not understand homework simply because she did not want to do it.

While many children will try to get out of doing homework when they can, for families of cross-cultural children the issue becomes even more difficult. Sometimes parents do not know the language and cannot help, or they cannot check up on the student to see that the work is completed as assigned. Roles in the family get shifted, and the child, because of more English ability, assumes more power by default. This shift naturally puts more burden on the family structure. In addition, in cross-cultural families, the students have even more reason to feel that the parents' ideas are not appropriate in a class with which the parents have little acquaintance. How students respond to these dilemmas naturally differs from one to the next; how teachers and parents can respond is to try to keep in closer touch, even through the use of a translator, if necessary.

In a comment surprising to me, Mrs. Torres shared her feelings about being a foreigner at the school. During the previous month, she had felt some hostility at Carina's school, particularly in comparison with her son's.

> At Carina's school, they don't seem to want foreigners. One day my husband was talking to the secretary at the school and she walked away while he was still talking to her. He got very upset and talked with the principal about it. However, we still feel that there is different treatment between the American-born children and other children. . . . In Riccardo's school, they help children from other countries, but in Carina's school, they don't. They call from Riccardo's school to see how he is doing, because he did not do well on his first test. My husband wrote something to the teacher, and the teacher called to say, "Thank you," and that Riccardo was doing better at school. They pay no attention like that to Carina at her school, except the ESL teacher. . . . Even though my husband wrote to Carina's teacher asking her to write if there was anything he needed to know, she doesn't do it. We must go constantly and ask. (Parent interview, November 4)

Mrs. Torres did try to balance the scales a bit by saying that Carina was not doing her fair share by being a good student. And she was quick to add that other than this point, life was filled with good things.

At the end of this parent interview, I asked Mrs. Torres if there was anything else she wanted to tell me. She said, with a smile, that she prayed a lot and that life got easier every day. I asked if she still thought that language was the biggest factor in the initial adjustment and she said, emphatically, "Yes!"

> Here, everything is easier than in Brazil. But I need to know English to know how to make the things easier—such as how to work the microwave. I can't read the directions! (Parent interview, November 4)

All four cross-cultural students had very supportive family systems. Despite their own issues of adjustment, the parents were able to take steps to help their children. For the sake of their children, parents sat with them to learn the class material, spent a lot of energy in looking for workable solutions, even took actions that were unfamiliar. They were very eager to know what their children were studying, but were unaccustomed to the ways of accomplishing that in the United States. When possible, they made trips to the schools to learn more about their children's adjustment, but sometimes met with what they interpreted as indifference. Many of the parents felt that additional contact was needed, particularly in the first three months, because neither they nor their children understood what was going on in school.

Notably, one theme that ran through the parents' interviews concerned the actual communication with the school. All parents mentioned the feeling of being overwhelmed by the flood of printed material from the schools at the beginning of the year; they often could not deal with it and put it aside at that time. Later, it became clear that the bulletins did not answer their particular questions concerning the specific content of the classes.

For the parents, knowing about their children's progress in school was very important; however, they could not always get this information from the children. In addition, it seemed to me that for parents accustomed to having children lug textbooks back and forth to school, the absence of that practice in U.S. elementary schools could result in further alienation of not knowing what was being taught in the classes, or which classes were being taught, or the goal of the methodology. Some of the parents' comments indicated concern with not only the smaller issues of homework or tests, but also larger arenas of the prevailing philosophy of education in the schools, procedures, the role of parents, and avenues for communication.

These parents were very involved in the acculturation of their children. They had the time and the resources to help their children—which did not seem to be utilized by the teachers. For any number of reasons, the opportunity to form a good alliance was missed. Instead, the parents felt urged to join the PTA, not by the teachers, but by the organization (and, in the parents' eyes, by the administration) itself. However, most parents did not sense real involvement in such an endeavor.

In a time when teachers in public schools are crying for more parental involvement in their child's education, there were four families who were ready to be very involved, but the connection never seemed to get made. The meaning of "parental support" differed between parents and teachers. The parents' expectations that home and school would be intricately involved seemed to be in sharp contrast to the teachers' expectations of a separation between home and school in an effort to help the child assume responsibility. This perceived attitude of the teachers was questioned by all of the parents.

TOWARD THE BEGINNING OF THE THIRD MONTH OF SCHOOL, DONNA HAD THIS to share about Carina:

> From the first day . . . Carina would have been twitching, or looking or whatever, skyward. And now, finally, she is beginning to tune in, because she knows, now, that I am going to call on her even if her hand isn't up. When I think she is capable of answering the question, if she is paying attention, I will call on her. She is the kind of child who will sit back as long as we let her. (Teacher interview, November 20)

In an observation in math class two and a half weeks later, I noticed that Carina's hand shot up for a number of the answers.

At the final interview with the teachers, fourteen weeks into the school year, Donna had this to say about Carina:

> Carina . . . is much more enthused, much more involved; she now wants her test back and, God love her, she thinks she is going to get an A, but she got only a 70. I know she is going to be upset, but there is nothing I can do about it. She did complete the test, which is interesting, because she hadn't in the past. That is not all that bad, given the fact that most of it she read on her own. But she is much more interested; she wants to know now the back work that she owes me. She wants a list of it so that she can work on it this weekend. That is a big difference. . . . She is much more invested.

Sheila added this comment:

> I have seen a difference in her awareness; she is a big helper. She will see me changing one of the animals and she will be right there; knows where to go for the chips and food.
>
> Donna: But she still calls us all "Teacher."
>
> JBC: Like we say, "Your Honor" to a judge . . .
>
> Donna and Sheila: Yeahhh! [laughter] (Teacher interview, December 16)

Asked what their definition of *adjustment* was, the teachers felt that it was different for different students.

> Sheila: I suppose you could say it was someone who feels comfortable.

Donna: For Carina, it is a sign of her adjustment that she is more in-vested now. . . .[Generally it is] [s]omeone who does their work, and who is part of the class, not an isolate, gets along with other kids. (Teacher interview, December 16)

Two days after this interview, I had the final interview with Carina. Ex-cept for her last two answers, all of the interaction between us was in English. Preliminary discussion focused on her having seen her homeroom teacher in a mall and on Christmas preparations in her home. A few sentences into reading *I Hate English,* the door opened and Sheila Dinesen walked in with Yevgeny in tow. She said, "Excuse me," to me and started talking to the trans-lator, asking her to please make sure that Yevgeny understood the directions for the Secret Elf game that they had been playing in her classroom for the past three days. Sheila felt that he had not understood the directions because he had not brought something in to share with his partner. I interrupted to say that this translator spoke Portuguese, not Russian.

Sheila Dinesen's action reflected her intense desire to help Yevgeny. Frustrated because she could not communicate well with him, she remem-bered only that a translator was in the next room. Although categorizing is a common human reaction, stereotyping must be guarded against. Uncon-sciously, we may lump into one group all those not in "our" group; for ex-ample, all of those in this classroom who do not speak English are in ESL classes. The fact that all of those in ESL classes do not speak each other's lan-guage, or that they have different abilities and needs, gets lost in the creation of that outgroup. Often ESL students are expected to be able to communicate with each other. Uniqueness becomes lost in the stereotyping.

After Sheila had left, I asked Carina what she thought was most impor-tant to know in a class in the United States, other than English. Her answer was, "Cooperation." When I asked if and how that might be played out with-out language, she said, "Yes, you can. Like the jacket I gave to Mary on the playground when she was cold. I didn't understand what she said, I just gave her my jacket." When asked if there was any final thought she wanted to share, she answered, in Portuguese, that life was much easier now:

I speak more English, so I can play more with my friends. Now they ask me to play with them; they didn't ask me before when I didn't speak En-glish. (Student interview, December 18)

This insight is important and points to the shifting status and balance of power as a result of knowing the language. Knowing English filled a primary social need and changed her relationships to a more equitable stance. Carina was looking forward to her birthday party in February when she might be able to invite her friends to her house.

LATER THAT AFTERNOON, I HAD THE FINAL INTERVIEW WITH HER PARENTS. Mrs. Torres commented on how pleased she was with Carina's progress in learning English. She had heard Carina talking with the ESL teacher and found that Carina understood everything the ESL teacher was saying. Carina had told her parents that she did not understand everything, but now that ruse, in the parents' eyes, had been discovered. Now that they realized the extent of her comprehension, they had stopped helping her with her homework. Mrs. Torres feared, however, that in the mainstream classes, when Carina did not understand something, she would not ask the teacher about it; she would simply let it slip by. Carina also was not responsible in bringing home notices from school. She had neglected to give her parents a notice about a PTA meeting the previous week. In a different vein, the mother added,

> Carina is very different now; she has changed a lot. She fights all the time with her father now. It makes her father sad; if he tells her to do something, she talks back. She is terrible. . . . She wants only to play, no responsibility. . . .She wants to argue all the time. . . . It has been increasing in the last three months. (Parent interview, December 18)

The process of acculturation is not just learning a language; it is also learning the values that underlie the culture or the behaviors that make sense in the culture. As such, it can involve a profound change in a person, particularly in children who want so much to be accepted by their peers. Value systems come into conflict, and the cross-cultural student and family are often the battleground.

When asked about their contact with the school and the teachers, Mrs. Torres said that she had accompanied her husband four times to school, but that he had had to go more often. She did not feel comfortable talking with the mainstream teachers. She felt that the ESL teacher was the only one who paid attention to her. The others just said, "Hi." From the Torres' perspective, the only thing that the PTA had done was to ask for money, and due to a mistake, the PTA had even asked them twice. The Torreses did not understand the role of the PTA. "They seem to call the parents they know and forget about the others. They are not going to worry about strangers."

My final question was about what the school could have done to have made it easier for Carina in the last three months. Mr. Torres' answer:

> I think the teachers could understand more the problem of students from other countries. Only the ESL teacher understands. (Parent interview, December 18)

Carina's relationship with me and others can be characterized by my last observation of her. The students had just come in from lunch recess and were milling about, waiting for their science teacher to return from lunch. Carina was in the midst of her friends. When I walked in, she saw me and immediately came over. We talked about the weather, the guinea pigs, and other little chitchat. Each time I had walked into her classroom, she had made contact with me, if not verbally (which was most often), at least visually and with a smile. Relationships with others were paramount for her. Her wish list, in her journal, was the following:

> I wish I knew enough English to talk to everybody and have more fun when we go to Florida. When I get back to Brazil, I wish I could bring my teacher with me. I wish to take all my friends in the classroom to Florida with me. (Student journal, November 17)

Yevgeny Mindlin

What I like about the school [in the United States] is the fact that the relationship between a teacher and a student is not necessarily like the one between a commanding officer and a soldier (as it was in Russia). And, generally speaking, here teachers do not have to introduce strict, Soviet army-like rules, in order to enforce discipline. So if I didn't have any "language problems" everything would have been awesome. . . . The only thing that I did not like was that everybody had to walk fast inside the school building. (I think it is ridiculous!) But the rest is "OK". This expression is used not only by Americans, so I knew it before. (Student journal, September, 1992)

*Y*evgeny Mindlin, his younger brother, Alexander, and their mother arrived in the United States less than a week before school began. Alexander was enrolled in the second grade of Valley School; Yevgeny was in the fifth grade, in the same section with Carina Torres, whose story was told in the previous chapter.

Mrs. Mindlin had been a biologist in Russia and had learned English in high school. Although she had not had much chance to use it in any way other than reading, she had continued to read biology books in English and to translate portions for colleagues at the school where she taught. She and her husband had been considering leaving Russia for some time. They had almost left for Israel, but canceled at the last minute. Although she was always in

64

favor of coming to the United States, her husband, who is older and does not have her facility in English, was not. He finally relented for the benefit of the children; she would come ahead with the children and he would stay behind to cope with various financial and business matters before joining them.

Yevgeny's parents did not tell him about the decision to move to the United States until close to the departure date. He said that he was not upset but "shocked" to hear of the decision, since his father and all his other relatives were to stay there. He did not know anything about the United States and hence did not have any expectations of what it would be like, other than skyscrapers, once they arrived. In Russia, the myth about the United States is that everyone is happy and wealthy.

> You can't compare American people to our people. In Russia everybody is drunk most of the time. . . . Women are always tired because they have to stay in line to get some food, and they have to spend all the time doing house chores. (Student interview, October 2)

The Mindlins had relatives in the United States who met them at the airport. Mrs. Mindlin had never met them because they were on her husband's side and had emigrated from Russia before she and her husband were married. They were most helpful in getting the Mindlins established in an apartment, in the community, and in Valley School. Mrs. Mindlin was determined not to rely on them too much because she wanted to learn better English and become independent as quickly as possible. This was evidenced by an attempt she related:

> I try talking on the phone as much as I can. I was trying to find a post office and I couldn't. No one was able to tell me where the nearest post office was. I tried looking in the "Yellow Pages" and they referred me to the "White Pages." Since I didn't know what the White Pages were, I couldn't look there. I called 411 [Information]. They gave me the phone number of a post office, which I called, but I couldn't make out the address they were giving me. (Parent interview, October 2)

She described her adjustment with the metaphor of feeling blind: She felt severed from her surroundings; she did not know where to go, where to find out about things. For example, public transportation was very difficult for her to figure out. It was hard to be the only adult in the family; she found that she often talked to her 10-year-old as a friend because he was older and could relate to the issues that were on her mind.

She was surprised by supermarkets that stay open 24 hours a day and have automatic doors that you do not "have to open with your nose" when your arms are full of bags, by ATM machines, by the use of checks for all sorts of payments, by trees and squirrels that were around her house. Her fears about the United States had been that she would not be able to find a decent place to live without smog, pollution, high-rise apartments, violence, and substandard schools for her children. She was extremely pleased with the living quarters the relatives had found for them. Even in three short weeks after her arrival, she had already looked through the Yellow Pages to find various environmental agencies that might produce job possibilities. She wanted to send them her resumé and visit them in person, because in the Russian culture a personal visit conveys the applicant's acknowledgment of the importance of the job, something not communicated by use of the phone. The T/EI commented that phones are not used extensively in Russia, particularly in business transactions. Interaction is more personalized.

At our initial interview, before the study started, Mrs. Mindlin and I sat in the sparsely furnished kitchen of a three-room, second-floor apartment in a three-unit, wooden building. Some trees between this dwelling and the one next to it afforded a pleasant view out of the kitchen window. During this initial interview, which was after school, five children were running very comfortably around the apartment. Mrs. Mindlin explained, with a smile, that only two were hers; the others were the children who lived downstairs. Their parents both worked, so the children often came up to the Mindlins immediately after school for a while.

Mrs. Mindlin commented on the different approaches of her two children during the first week of school: Alexander, in the second grade, was very social. He had been terrified and upset at being in school. Yevgeny, on the other hand, was "less into friends, more into books, into being with his parents" and somewhat more confident in his approach to school.

Yevgeny was a tall, thin, angular, studious boy with dark hair and dark purple-framed glasses. There was a stiffness about him that augured his lack of ease in social situations. He appeared to be a scholar.

> Generally [in Russia] I played only with my school friends who were in the same classroom with me. It happened because of a number of reasons: (1) Unfortunately I'm not a very social person; (2) I did not like to spend my free time in the yard; and finally (3) I was busy most of the time (I had school, numerous homework assignments, flute lessons, and solfeggio) (November 3). . . . After the best student in my class moved to another country, I became the best student in my class and I am very proud of it. (Student journal, November 10)

As a result of their good academic records in their native countries, all of the cross-cultural students in this study arrived with strong self-images, particularly as students. Their academic excellence meant that they were able to perform well in those classes where language facility was not paramount (e.g., particularly math and some science). They threw themselves into the study of English, and most of them tried to do what was expected of them in other classes where they could manage the language. They had been good students and expected to continue as such.

In some ways, however, this strong self-image became a negative force: Because the children were accustomed to doing well, they expected a lot of themselves, and hence they became very discouraged when they did not measure up. For those who had friends to help assuage the feelings of frustration and failure, it was a little easier to bear than for those who were shy.

SHY AND VERY COMPETENT, YEVGENY HAD ATTENDED A PRIVATE JEWISH SCHOOL in his homeland, having transferred there from a public school.

> In school I had a friend whose name was Lenny. We both had been in school since the day it opened three years before. (In our classroom there were only five people left who started the school at the same time I did. The rest emigrated.) Very often Lenny acted weird, but generally he was a typical Soviet boy (November 3). In Russia we had breaks after each lesson. But generally we went outside during breaks, too, although there we did not have an excellent playground. (Student journal, October 27)

His mother explained further in her journal:

> Yevgeny started his first grade in one of the "standard" ordinary schools in Leningrad. He was in a mediocre first-grade class. . . . He could read and count before he started school and after acquiring writing skills, . . . he seemed to be bored and uninterested in school. I decided to take him out of school. He passed the final exams of the second grade without attending classes and was accepted in the third grade of a newly organized Hebrew school in Leningrad. (Parent journal, September 19)

Yevgeny's memories of his first day at Valley School were memorable for reasons more significant to him than to his teachers:

> I can only talk about my first part of my first day in school—that is, about the time before I actually went to my classroom. Parents are not allowed to ride on the school bus and so I didn't take a school bus because my parents had to come with me to fill out some forms. Instead our relatives gave us a ride to the school. By the time we finished filling out necessary forms, the classes had already started and I was 10 minutes late. Then I remember the teacher showing me my locker and my desk

and telling me that Lara speaks Russian. I also remember asking Lara what I was supposed to do. During snack time my classmates shared food with me because I didn't know that I was supposed to bring snack to school. I didn't understand anything during the lessons. I even could not understand what lessons existed in American schools. (Student journal, November 5)

The primary challenge that these four cross-cultural students felt was that of learning English. By choice or default, these students were in an ESL program, not a bilingual program that would have afforded them the support of a linguistic reference group. Their parents stated repeatedly in interviews their feelings that the children would learn the language best by being surrounded by it. The students, themselves, commented that having English-speaking friends would help them learn the language faster.

There were academic purposes to learning the language: Integration into the work of the class would come faster. The students had all demonstrated their strong desire to become integrated quickly into the class, and for that, language was needed. They stated in later interviews that they were pleased with the linguistic improvement they had made. As the interviews progressed, they were eager to show that they could not only understand but also answer some of the interview questions in English.

Learning the language, however, was for more than just academic purposes; it also was for social purposes, a very important need for these students. Even Carina, who was able to make friends easily, commented that her relationships changed as she got to know the language better; that is, she was *sought out* more when she knew the language better. For the gregarious students, learning the language meant more friends, which, in turn, meant learning the language faster. For the shy students, the spiral slowed and almost degenerated as language developed at a much slower pace.

When asked further in his first interview about his first day at Valley School, Yevgeny added that he had felt a little lonely that day. On the second and third days, he was a little uncomfortable, but by the fourth, he had started to feel that he "was fitting into the environment where he was." He played mostly with Lara (a compatriot and classmate) and with Carina.

His mother wrote also of the paperwork in the school's administrative office:

The first day of school was very difficult for all of us. My children are at an age where they tend to copy the behavior of their classmates; they want to do what "everybody else is doing." So, the fact that they could not go directly to their classrooms with the other students and had to wait in the office until all the paperwork was done, threw them off balance completely. Alexander was so upset that an ESL teacher had to calm him down before taking him to his second-grade class. (Parent journal, September 19)

ON MY INITIAL VISIT TO THE VALLEY SCHOOL, WHEN I WAS MAKING THE FIRST CONTACT with the ESL teacher and the principal, I also happened to meet Sheila Dinesen, who was the homeroom/science teacher for Yevgeny and Carina. Sheila had had six years of teaching experience abroad, with numerous ESL students in her classes there. After I explained, in generalities, about my study, she commented,

> He is a most unusual child. He is going to have a lot of trouble acclimating. . . . He is simply not focusing on work at all. He won't do anything. He is not there; he has a glazed look. The other student is fine. She'll come up to me and say, "I no understand." I can deal with that.

Two days later, after I had had the meeting with the participating teachers to obtain their consent to take part in my research, Donna Devereaux, the math teacher, sought me out and commented on how well she thought Yevgeny was doing, that he really wanted to participate, that you could "see" him doing the math problem in Russian and then translating it into English. At this point, math required less language facility than did science or homeroom activities.

Given these initial assessments, it was not a total surprise to hear the comments of the teachers at their first interview a month later, during lunch in the Teachers' Room. Asked to talk about both cross-cultural students' first days in school, they launched into a lengthy discussion about Yevgeny and his social distance from his peers:

> Donna: He is far more into academics than she [Carina]. I haven't talked to Yevgeny's parents; he comes in with his work; he seems to be trying. . . . I think he is a lot like a number of other kids we have had who came out of Russia. I think he is very bright. My experience with them is that often they are very proud and . . . most of them came from schools where they were very good and they do not like not being good. . . . He answers, raises his hand; he pretty much has the numbers now so he can. He's the kind of kid who won't talk to anybody until he can speak in full sentences. We have had kids like that before; they are primarily Russian Jews who often have been excellent academically where they came from, and all of a sudden they find themselves at the bottom of the barrel and they don't know how to communicate to the kids. . . . It takes them a while, more so in some ways than others, to get acclimated in terms of social skills.

Sheila countered,

> I find Yevgeny very, extremely, really extremely withdrawn. I don't want
> to say antisocial; he has a right to be antisocial since he doesn't know the
> language . . . [but] he makes no effort to communicate. . . . I think he is
> very, very scared. (Teacher interview, October 14)

When asked if they had ever had the experience of native-born children who
were studious and withdrawn or who had difficulty mixing in, they felt that
Yevgeny's situation seemed to be more extreme, that there were usually other
extenuating circumstances. Sheila commented that she longed to see a smile
now and then.

We continued with a discussion about whether cross-cultural students
had had any impact on their teaching styles. Generally the feeling was that
teaching styles did not change; lesson modification happened with anyone
who did not understand; the difference for these students was the availability
of either a peer translator or an ESL teacher who might help.

Teaching styles in the classrooms of this study were fairly different than
the ones to which the cross-cultural students were accustomed. Most had
come from cultures that had been much more formal, teacher-oriented,
transmission-model teaching. Here in Winsted, small-group instruction, a
hands-on, experiential approach, the absence of textbooks, and no oral examinations or recitations were all new approaches for these students. They
found it a surprise, albeit pleasant, to be taught in such a manner. Accustomed to proving their abilities by memorization of material, this new experiential way did not always seem like learning. They felt the need to somehow
prove their capabilities but were unable to do so.

Another difference keenly felt by Yevgeny, as evidenced by the number
of times it came up in the interviews, was the emphasis, and yet limits, on
cooperation.

> Here, you don't help other children; you don't cheat on exams; you don't
> cheat on your papers; you can't just copy the paper of another kid. When
> some kid is answering a question, you can't help him. In Russia, it is very
> popular. Kids will cheat. It is considered normal. Here, even among kids,
> it is not considered accepted. (Student interview, October 2)

The distinction between cooperation and cheating was new for some of these
cross-cultural students. Not having had the experience of group work before,
it was hard for some of them to understand the parameters of working together. Yevgeny continued with his assessment:

> Children here help each other more in a legitimate way. There was some
> of that in my Jewish school, but it is more here. In my science class, I sit

with three other people, one is Lara. . . . They don't help me with anything in science class; they are not mean, but the situation never happened for us to communicate. I don't need a lot of help in science, just translation from Lara. . . . The other kids didn't talk to me because they knew I didn't understand English and . . . I didn't talk with them because I knew that they would not understand me. (Student interview, October 16)

Mrs. Mindlin wrote in her journal about the differences:

A lot of things in school are new for my kids. Cooperation, one of the important principles of education promoted here, is completely new for Soviet children. In Soviet schools, cooperation is not encouraged. Every student has to work independently and any cooperation among students is prohibited. Children are not allowed to talk to each other or consult each other's notes while working on the same project. This rule is, however, frequently broken by students. (Parent journal, September 19)

Yevgeny, a top student in Russia, was accustomed to working independently. That background made this challenge of group work all the more difficult. In addition to the amount and complexity of language involved in cooperative learning, some students must also be introduced to the *concept*. Nevertheless, it is a methodology that is generally very beneficial to most cross-cultural students as they work with peers to arrive at answers. Small groups provide more support, more focus, more security, and more accessibility to understanding than does large-group instruction. The desks in Yevgeny's classrooms were arranged into groups and, in math, where a little less language was required, Donna Devereaux pointed out that as the children began to understand his math abilities, they turned to him more and more for cooperative problem solving.

Teachers also teach to the different learning modalities (auditory, visual, kinesthetic) of their students. Strategies that are visual and kinesthetic are particularly helpful for cross-cultural students. For example, to see written (on the board) that which is being discussed helps the cross-cultural student follow the topic. Spoken words may be lost as soon as they are expressed, whereas written words, signs, and symbols can provide an extended resource. This does not mean that all communication needs to be in writing (even as it is not for the visual learner), but that using such props as an overhead projector, pictures, pointing, and key words written on the board are particularly helpful, especially during the first few months of a cross-cultural student's life in the classroom.

In addition to the impact on their teaching styles, I asked the teachers about the impact of the cross-cultural students on the class. The social studies teacher was excited to have had a student a few years before who had lived close to the area of the Chernobyl incident, who could speak of it first hand.

Sheila: But then, you can't do that kind of thing until they can communicate better than these kids can. . . . On the first day of school, when I
plotted where everyone was from on our class map, I put them way off
the map because it is of America, and my kids knew what was going on,
but they [the cross-cultural students] didn't. But it couldn't be much of
a dialogue. There is not much communication at this point. (Teacher
interview, October 14)

While Sheila was looking forward to verbal interaction with these students,
we must remember that there is a lot of nonverbal communication taking
place. In the incident she described, it is unfortunate that a world map was
unavailable because of the unintended nonverbal message sent that Russia
and Brazil were beyond the scope of importance in this class. In addition,
cross-cultural students, even without language, can open the eyes of their
peers and teachers to life, values, and behaviors of a different culture and can
be catalysts in the development of attitudes of mainstream students toward
those who are different linguistically, physically, mentally, emotionally, culturally, and ethnically. One impact of the cross-cultural students on their
peers came up during this discussion:

Donna: It's interesting, like all kids that come out of the Soviet system,
when he goes to answer a question—he's breaking himself . . .

Sheila: What do you mean "he's breaking himself"?

Donna: He is breaking himself of doing this [standing up to answer]. . . .
Those are the kinds of things he has to learn which set him apart from
other kids, and the kids look at him like, "Ohhh, is he weird."

Sheila: That is good for the kids to know, I think, that in other cultures
class is conducted in different ways. That is good. (Teacher interview,
October 14)

The relationship between Lara (a compatriot who had been in the United
States for about three years) and Yevgeny, and the teachers' expectations of that
common bond to the homeland, was then explored by the teachers:

Sheila: I always have to ask Lara to translate. If there is something that I
really feel Yevgeny needs to know, even though I sat them across from
each other on purpose, Lara will never . . . say to him, "Hey, by the way,
that means that you have to bring in your dollar tomorrow." Every now
and then I catch myself and say, "Oh, Lara, will you please tell him that
this is important?"

Donna: Because she is new. I think you are putting a lot of burden on
her. She is still feeling her way in this school. . . . [Though she was in the

system for the past two years], she is moving into a new school. She wants social acceptance here, and she is trying to feel her way. To be tagged with a new kid . . . in a way her reaction is normal. . . . If Lara were a more accepted part of this group and had been with these kids for a number of years, and therefore had a place and felt she had a place, then she would be more willing. (Teacher interview, October 14)

Donna Devereaux's feeling was that the children who had come up through the grades together had built a cohesiveness and a base of security out of which they could reach out to others. Lara had no such base, and in her own way, as a new student, was still struggling. Sheila continued to use Lara as a translator, but less frequently, and asked her instead whether she thought that Yevgeny had understood.

The difference between the teachers' expectations of the translator and Lara's perception of her role became evident during an observation in science when I overheard Lara commenting to a peer that he should talk directly to Yevgeny; she refused to answer for him.

Yevgeny's dependence on Lara's translation was a part of his journal entries during the first month of school:

I understand what is going on only when my Russian friend interprets for me . . . or when I can figure things out using my mental abilities (too bad it doesn't happen very often). The rest of the time I do not know what is going on in the class. I do not understand explanations in social studies, in math (which, thank God, I learned in my Russian school), and partly in science. I do not understand music completely and library is absolutely useless time spent for me. But generally I consider myself lucky; I can explain myself in English although I have trouble understanding English that is spoken to me and there is a person in my class who can interpret for me. (Student journal, undated, sometime before October 15)

THE FIRST DAY I OBSERVED YEVGENY, THE EIGHTH DAY OF SCHOOL, HE WAS IN MATH class; he did not acknowledge my presence in any way. When the teacher asked the students to get out their homework so that it could be corrected by a deskmate, Yevgeny spoke to her and went back to his seat with the book. While the children were correcting, the book was open in front of him and he was looking at it diligently. Now and then he would write something. He never looked up. After the correction of homework, the class was asked to open their books. Yevgeny was reminded to direct his attention to the book; he had been briefly gazing out the window and playing with the radiator. When the extra sheet of homework was passed out, in addition to the assignment in the book, Yevgeny was ahead of all the others, able to perform that which was requested in the problems.

A few days later, I was back in math class. About halfway into the period, the class started locating gridpoints through word problems. Donna was standing by the overhead projector, reading the problem and asking for volunteers for the answers. Yevgeny's interest seemed to flag a great deal at this point. His shoulders drooped, he started playing with his pencil. Carina (at a different set of desks) had her head on her arms on the desk. After a little while, I walked over to Yevgeny's side and started to point to the gridpoints that Donna was talking about. As she saw me do this, Donna moved over to Carina and started pointing out things to her. In that way, both children were able to catch on to what was going on in class and actually participated in some of the answers.

Although Yevgeny was able to follow along in math class, other classes were more difficult for him. One day, during homeroom, Yevgeny busied himself with the section of the science project that was to copy sketches of pond creatures. He was absorbed in what he was doing, totally focused, bent over intently studying the sketches. On another day, during language arts, a different picture emerged. When I arrived, the teacher was in the Author's Corner, with the children assembling around her on the rug. Yevgeny was on the rug, sitting on his heels, but behind the only chair that was on the rug, out of the view of the teacher, his back turned toward her. A boy was sitting on the chair. During the interview following this observation, when asked for further understanding about this seemingly hostile stance, Yevgeny became very uncomfortable and, according to the T/EI, did not like the question at all; she wondered how or if she could have phrased it differently so that he would not have been so upset by it. She had included, as part of the question, the fact that often he looked at his book instead of the teacher. Was this an easier way to understand for him? He responded by saying that since he did not understand what the teacher was saying, he saw no reason to look at her; he repeated many times that he liked the teacher. The T/EI thought that he seemed scared by the question.

When his mother was asked if he had mentioned his feelings about his teachers to her, she replied,

> [Alexander and Yevgeny] love the ESL teacher. I think Yevgeny likes his homeroom teacher. It is very difficult for him to distinguish the teacher from the person, so since he doesn't understand a lot of what is going on in her classroom, he may feel uneasy about her as a person, because he cannot take apart the person and the teacher. He sees her as a teacher who is not very happy that he does not understand something. But on the other hand, he likes her. (Parent interview, November 13)

In this second interview with Yevgeny, at about the fifth week of school, the questions had been of a more personal nature than they had been in the first—for example, about his behavior in class, life in St. Petersburg, his feelings on his progress in English. The T/EI felt that it had been a very difficult interview for him. She had had to work very hard to get this usually reflective, articulate boy to talk. He commented that he missed his father, St. Petersburg, the museums, the river Neva, and all of the cultural elements of the city. He also missed "his people," by which he did not mean his family or friends, but more, a sense of being able to anticipate another's responses:

> When you're in Russia, you know what to expect of people, and here I don't really know. I can't tell what people are going to do or what should be the response. From the one side, they are smiling and very polite, and then on the other side, they put their feet on the desk, which is totally unacceptable in a Soviet school. (Student interview, October 2)

Shortly after this interview, his mother wrote in her journal about the difficult adjustment that Yevgeny's brother was having and one of the ways in which she was trying to help both children:

> Today after classes we went to "our" river that has a bridge over it and a dam. We love the view of the river from the bridge, although we "discovered" it just a couple of days ago. There are two waterfalls, cliffs, and hemlocks on one side of the river and woods on the other side. The view is spectacular! To see all this "genuine" nature right around the corner from my own house—sounds unbelievable. The kids love the bridge and the view from it. And indeed it is quite a bridge. It's huge and . . . so beautiful and clean that it seems as though it was built only for us. There is something surrealistic about this bridge. (Parent journal, October 6)

The following weekend, the mother and sons took two special trips: one to a special museum for children and the other to an aquarium.

THROUGHOUT THE STUDY, YEVGENY ARTICULATED DIFFERENCES BETWEEN Valley School and his school in Russia. One was the sense of "disorganization" that he felt in the classroom in the United States. That everybody could walk around during class and yet be productive was remarkable to him. He said that in Russia, students were not allowed out of their seats without permission. Another difference he noticed was

> in terms of discipline. There [in Russia] the teacher will say something and the student has to do that. And here, it is more the teacher will give you direction and then you can choose. (Student interview, October 2)

His mother wrote in her journal about Yevgeny's surprise at the lack of rules in the classroom:

> After his first day in school, Yevgeny told us about the cage with guinea pigs. After one guinea pig had a baby, the teacher put a sign on the cage which said, "Don't touch us." "And indeed nobody touches them!" said my son with puzzlement. (Parent journal, September 25)

Yevgeny also commented on his amusement and surprise at calling a teacher by her last name, and his delight at the cleanliness of the school:

> I don't have to change from outdoor shoes to indoor shoes. Frankly, I don't understand how I will be without indoor shoes when the winter comes. (Student journal, December 2)

Another difference was in the physical education class. Mrs. Mindlin had high hopes for this class. Both she and Yevgeny had had doubts about it at first, because in Russia physical education had not been his favorite period. Tests had been required of the students, and Yevgeny, not being very athletic, had had a hard time measuring up. He had been afraid that he would be required to do pull-ups on a trapeze, which he would be unable to perform. The emphasis in Winsted on fitness, enjoyment, and skills achieved through games made physical education very popular with Yevgeny. In addition, Mrs. Mindlin commented that the short commands used in physical education enabled her children to understand what was going on. She was pleased that they could tell her all the rules of the games when they came home. Yevgeny's enjoyment of this new-found interest was evident by the number of times he mentioned it in his journal. For example, asked to "tell about something that made you happy this week," he wrote,

> Good things that happened last week ... We won a game of soccer. The score was three to zero. I didn't score, but it didn't matter.
>
> My ESL teacher got the paper for the printer, which means that we can use the computer again. (Student journal, October 29)

DURING THE SECOND WEEK OF SCHOOL, THE MUSIC/CHORUS TEACHER HAD COMMENTED on how Yevgeny had participated in a game that had involved getting up and moving to another chair. He had not asked or answered questions, which were part of the game, but he "had understood the directions" enough to grab a chair. During the fifth week of school, she discovered that Yevgeny's name was not on her chorus seating chart. She asked him how to spell it and he answered her clearly and deliberately, with no prompting. Yevgeny participated in chorus by singing along as best he could. During the seventh week of school, the chorus teacher had been doing an exercise in which the pianist stopped playing in the middle of a musical phrase to see if the students could identify where she had stopped. On the fourth one, Yevgeny's hand went up, barely, about shoulder height. I think he was surprised when he was called on. The music teacher said, "Yevgeny, can you tell us where we stopped? . . . [pause] . . . Well, you probably don't understand and don't have enough English to tell us," and then called on another person. Yevgeny looked crestfallen. When asked about this during an interview after the incident, he said that he knew what the answer was, but that he was having trouble formulating the response in English.

In art class, Yevgeny sat at a long table with just one other student—at the other end. The art teacher was commenting on the drawings of the previous week as she was returning them: Yevgeny's needed to be bigger. Most of the students who needed to redo the project took another sheet of paper and started over. Yevgeny's behavior, however, hinted at a mindset tuned to scarcity and conservation of resources: He simply drew the larger picture on the same page, knowing that the smaller object would be incorporated into the design of the larger. While Carina had enjoyed the sociability this class afforded, Yevgeny worked alone and enjoyed the product of his effort.

In library, although he said it was fairly useless, Yevgeny was able to follow along in skill-related classes in a limited fashion, completing parts of the activities that were assigned. One of his first times in the library, when allowed to search for books to read for pleasure, he rejected other suggestions in favor of *Alice in Wonderland*. He said that he had read it in Russian and thought he could read it now in English with his mother, but he returned it without reading it. His perspective on these classes:

> I love physical education. We are doing jump ropes now; we played games for a while, but now we are working with jump ropes. I don't have to do ten pushups and be graded on that. . . . Art is easier than others [music, library] because I can understand almost everything in art. . . . Music, I don't dislike it, but I don't like it very much. I don't understand a lot. . . . I liked practicing for the Thanksgiving concert more than performing in it. . . . In library I have nothing to do. For 45 minutes the teacher lectures about books and I don't understand anything at all. Last time, when we could take books out, I heard the teacher mention the name of a book, so I got it out to read to my first-grade partner. I took it home and liked it. . . . [Asked if he had read it to his brother, he answered with a smile,] "No, it was the other way around; he read it to me." (Student interview, December 4)

In addition to physical education, ESL was Yevgeny's favorite class. He felt comfortable with the teacher and the demands of the class, and he particularly enjoyed the computer. In one of my visits there, he volunteered to show me some of the compositions he had written. When I observed the class, he was very diligent and focused on his work; his enjoyment and excitement of being able to understand the material was evident in his somewhat more relaxed body language. His mother corroborated his attitude:

> The teacher is kind; she is smiling all the time. Another factor that attracts them to ESL is that they have a computer there. And also, the assignments are easier for them, they can complete them. (Parent interview, November 13)

In addition to teaching the ESL curriculum, the ESL teacher was there to help the cross-cultural students adjust to some of the demands of their other classes. Later in the semester, when they had rejoined the social studies class, writing a report proved to be a new and difficult experience for Yevgeny and Carina, as it is with many cross-cultural students, not only in terms of the complexity of language required, but also in terms of the cultural expectations and the organizational patterns of formal reports. In addition to observable behaviors that we attribute to culture, there is a vast array of implicit, assumed, learned patterns that people from all cultures acquire and take for granted. For example, not all cultures write in the same format of organization or style that is used in the United States.

ALONG WITH ESL, TWO GOOD THINGS HAPPENED FOR YEVGENY AT ABOUT THE fifth and sixth weeks:

> I have passed the math test. Thank God, I was able to translate all the problems and got 100%. At phys. ed. class we beat the red jerseys. It was some kind of a new game. They didn't score, but we scored a triple. (Student journal, October 15)

A week later, I had barely gotten my coat off in science class when Sheila called me over to hear Yevgeny list the parts of a microscope, which was one of the procedures required for the science unit. He did it well and Sheila congratulated him with a handshake. Jared followed suit. Ted, who happened to sit next to Yevgeny said, "Hey, Yevgeny, give me a 'high five'!" which Yevgeny knew how to do, and did. Shortly thereafter, I started to inquire of Sheila whether a friendship might be forming between Ted and Yevgeny and began,

"I noticed . . . ," which she then completed with, ". . . his thick accent?"

Her comment again focuses attention on the importance of spoken language for this teacher. While learning the language is important, as judged by the cross-cultural students themselves as well as the teachers, it is crucial that the other aspects (e.g., learning "high fives" and figuring out strategies to make friends) of acculturation not be dismissed or ignored. A teacher's attitude toward these steps is as crucial as the support for language learning.

At the end of their science class on that brisk fall day, the teacher allowed the students an extra, short recess. Most ran out to play "Capture the Flag." While Carina seemed to know the rules, or at least stood in the middle of the field running around, Yevgeny stood awkwardly at the sidelines, watching the game, looking up to the sky, then wandering over to the jungle gym where another group of children had gathered. Sheila explained that the previous week she had asked the boys to try to include him in their games, which they had generously done that day but apparently had not carried over to today. When she blew the whistle, signaling the children to come inside, Yevgeny was the first one in the door, even before she realized that he had gone in.

SCIENCE CONTINUED TO PRESENT A PARTICULAR CHALLENGE TO YEVGENY. THE class had taken a field trip to a nearby pond and returned with pond water to analyze under a microscope. His entry into his journal reflected some of his frustration:

> Thanks to Carina I finally got the creatures, and now I can do some things for my science. After several days the creatures almost died, because somebody from another class drained almost all the water. I poured some tap water on them and they seemed to pull through. (Student journal, October 15)

Sheila's interview revealed a totally different perspective on the same activity, but the same sense of frustration:

> I guess I'd say he "is making satisfactory progress." He seems to know enough to come to me and ask a question by the tone in his voice or the look in his eye. . . . I think he feels more a part of the class now.
>
> JBC: Has ESL had an influence on that?
>
> Sheila: No, I think it is his acclimation to the classroom. . . . I don't think it has anything to do with mastery of English, because he hasn't mastered anything. . . . I'll point to the procedures that he should do of the science project and have Lara explain. He shouldn't be just drawing creatures, but every time I go over, he's drawing creatures. . . . I don't see him doing anything but looking at the creatures. I don't see him looking to

his peers or coming to me and asking me to interpret one of his activities. But I'm not asking him to do many of these. If he wants to sit there and intricately draw these creatures, that's all right. . . . He's pretty self-sufficient. When he doesn't know what to do, he "mucks out" with the pond water, with the hand magnifier, the microscope, the drawings. (Teacher interview, October 28)

From these two perspectives of the same event, one can see the miscommunication that was occurring. There were the practicalities: Yevgeny was trying to keep the creatures alive; Sheila was looking for progress on the procedures. Unaccustomed to having to ask the teacher for help, unsure of his English, innately shy, he tried to go it alone. She had many other students who needed her attention. However, there was also, perhaps, an underlying difference in expectations. Sheila was giving him room to make his own decisions and chart his own course in accomplishing the assigned tasks. Yevgeny, on the other hand, coming from a more structured classroom background, may have been hoping for more direction, less laissez-faire. Both student and teacher were working out of their best intentions but were missing each other.

MATH, HOWEVER, WAS NOT A PROBLEM. DONNA COMMENTED,

He is doing all of the work that is expected of him. All of the regular fifth grade work. . . . He is getting a little more comfortable. He will actually talk occasionally to someone in the class about something. He will try to get some help. He will go to a kid if I am not available. But I haven't seen too much change yet. (Teacher interview, October 28)

Unfortunately for Yevgeny, the joy of having mastered the parts of a microscope in English soon faded:

Generally bad things happen to me less often than good ones. This week, however, was the exception because I failed the science test. I just did not know that I was supposed to know the names of all the creatures living in a pond. Sure enough, I got less than 68%. Now I'm sitting at the table and studying for the re-examination. (Student journal, November 12)

During his interview on the day following that entry, Yevgeny talked about having lost a game in physical education, about how different class pictures in the United States were from those in Russia; he could not imagine a Russian class posing all over a jungle gym for their class picture. His responses to the SSPS pictures were extensive (only parts of his responses are quoted here). He identified the first picture (of the classroom, with a teacher at a desk) as definitely being a Russian classroom because the teacher's desk was right next to the blackboard, and the desk was devoid of all but a few blank sheets of paper. That the student had his hands in his pockets, however, made him think that perhaps it was not Russia, but there were too many other factors to change his mind. The expression on the child's face indicated that he was a mediocre student; had he been a good student he would have been happy to be there:

> The teacher said, "Ivanoff, go to the blackboard." ... He did not volunteer to come to the teacher's desk. After this, he will answer, somehow, something, whatever, just to get back to his seat. Then he will go back to his seat, happy that it is over, maybe not happy with his answer, but happy that it is over.

The picture of the playground, with one boy on the sidelines watching three boys playing with a ball, was a soccer game:

> [T]hese three boys had a bad attitude toward this one boy and this ... boy was angry at somebody that he was not accepted in the game; maybe he was angry at the boys or maybe he was angry at himself. It was probably the boy's own fault that he was not accepted in the game, but maybe he tried to do his best but it turned out to be the worst. That sometimes happens; you wish for the best but it turns out the worst. After the picture, the three will go someplace together, because now is not the time for making up [with the fourth].

The third picture was of a boy sitting at a table with two books to the side and one open in front of him:

> The main feeling of this boy is, "God, let me finish, let me memorize all this." ... The two books that are closed he had not read yet, because otherwise he would look much happier that he was finished with those books, too. Those two books are either too hard for him or too boring, or maybe both; maybe they are boring because they are hard. He can't understand them. The textbook that is open is math; he is doing problem solving.

Yevgeny thought that perhaps the student in that picture, who hadn't liked the assignment the teacher had given, might not study very hard because he did not look determined. But then, he gave it further thought and added

> Well, I was in a similar situation with the science test, and I thought that I would never be able to finish it ... so maybe this boy will pull through. So, even though he has an unhappy, undetermined face, he will solve all the problems.

The final picture, of the family in an office, was guessed as a principal's office. The family was there to register their son for school.

> And the boy is feeling uneasy. I know the feeling quite well, because when I am taken to places that I am unfamiliar with, I feel uneasy too. It is an uncomfortable feeling. . . . The family has to wait for a long time for the principal. . . . After that they do all the paperwork, and then he goes to either first or second grade. (Student interview, November 13)

Yevgeny commented at this interview that he felt that his English was improving; he felt that he talked more and that much of his passive English was turning into active English. When I asked the T/EI about the use of "passive" and "active," she responded that Yevgeny had used those words; he had probably picked them up from his mother, with whom the T/EI had talked the previous day, and had heard her use the same expression. Yevgeny thought that it would help him a lot if he had a friend who spoke only English. He didn't have that person yet, but he would like to.

YEVGENY HAD A BROAD SMILE ON HIS FACE WHEN I PICKED HIM UP FOR AN interview in mid-November, the beginning of the third month of school. As we left, Sheila saw the smile and celebrated it, commenting that it was the first smile she had seen since the beginning of school. She exclaimed, "You have made my day!" as he walked out of class. When we got to the room and I explained what the interchange had been about, Yevgeny explained that in Russian schools, students are not supposed to smile; it is not common to smile. In the middle of his interview, Sheila burst in with his science retest: He had gotten an A, only one wrong. He was delighted—and smiled again. Sheila told him that she was also delighted to have seen him smile twice in one day.

The importance to various teachers of this nonverbal communicative act points to some underlying values in U.S. elementary classrooms. A happy atmosphere in the classroom is evident as a priority of elementary teachers. Great effort and long hours are spent making their classrooms pleasant places, designing creative lessons to make all students comfortable, engaged, and cheerful. The underlying philosophy is that learning should be fun; it need not be tedious or repetitive. The emphasis on fun, on being happy, and, additionally, on being entertained, is a reflection of the values of the larger society. Kimball (1963) has said that the three main values of U.S. culture are self-fulfillment, change, and optimism. These three, and increasingly, that of being entertained, can be seen in many activities in the classroom. If we consider just the value of optimism, we can see that when teachers are unable to converse with cross-cultural students, they must rely on nonverbal communication to read their students' feelings and progress. In this study, getting the student to smile, that is, to communicate what the teachers saw as some positive interaction, became very important. Erik's teacher had tried to get him to smile on his first day, after his tenuous beginning. Carina's teachers commented on her pretty smile and how her frequent use of it indicated that "she would do all right." Yevgeny's teacher felt that there had been a breakthrough when he had actually smiled in class.

It cannot be overemphasized that the meaning attached to various acts of nonverbal behavior is not the same from culture to culture. Early in my career as an ESL teacher, I used to repeat a poster I had once seen (I blush even now as I am writing this sentence): A smile is the same in every language. It was only as I took courses in cross-cultural awareness that I realized that my Japanese students weren't necessarily exhibiting joy about being in my classes. In their culture, a smile can also hide embarrassment. Eager to find evidence of adjustment, I had used the interpretation that my culture gives to a smile and assumed it meant they were adjusting and happy. This is not to say that behaviors can't have the same meaning; it *is* to say that we must not assume that they do. In addition, as we have seen, while not a major adjustment, the cross-cultural students may experience some dissonance in trying to apply their seriousness of study to "fun" activities.

Furthermore, nonverbal communication has a two-way nature about it: Even as the teacher looks to the student for a nonverbal sign (a smile), so the student tries to read the teacher and peers. It is vital to remember that much more communication is nonverbal than verbal. Teachers must be alert to the messages sent to the cross-cultural students through the gamut of their and the peers' behaviors (e.g., tone of voice, exclusion from class tasks, from a map, from a group, from extra help, etc.). Already feeling tenuous due to lack of English, the cross-cultural students may attach more meaning to these acts than is intended.

ADJUSTMENT ISSUES CONTINUED AT HOME, WHERE YEVGENY'S MOTHER WAS having to adjust to being on the outside of her children's experiences. In the second interview with her, she shared her feelings that the children did not tell her much about life in school. The common answers to her queries about the day were that the children did not remember or that nothing happened. Apparently her hunch became evident with the first science test, which Yevgeny had failed. Only after the fact did he ask for her help, saying, "I have to work on this test and I don't know how to do it."

However, she did feel that the adjustment to living in the United States and to English was coming along well. Yevgeny was enrolled in Hebrew school and had to get there on his own three times a week; the walk to the temple took 45 minutes. Mrs. Mindlin and her younger son went to pick up Yevgeny after class, since it was dark by then. Despite his fluency in Hebrew, he seemed to be as quiet there as he was at Valley School until his mother found out about his reticence and worked on boosting his confidence. Later in his journal, in answer to the cue to "tell . . . something special that has happened to you since your arrival in the U.S.A.," Yevgeny wrote the following:

> Not so long ago I made a clay menorah in the studio of the Jewish Community Center. A man who explained how to do it was a real sculptor. After I made my menorah, I colored it. It turned out OK. Then we turned in our work and drove back to Hebrew school. (Student journal, December 4)

One month later, by the time of the final interview with Mrs. Mindlin, she could tell the translator and me that Yevgeny was no longer afraid to take the bus to Hebrew school on his own. The difference between the transit systems here and in Russia had scared him; he was not confident of where he needed to alert the driver that he wanted to get off. He could now do that. A further indication of adjustment was that both children, by the final interview, were able to run errands at the grocery store on their own.

> They both go shopping on their own and they both love it very much, although they are both saying that in America kids don't go food shopping on their own. But, they like it a lot and they go shopping for me, do small errands. (Parent interview, December 14)

Yevgeny's trip to Hebrew School and forays to the supermarket also mirrored the amount of responsibility entrusted to children in the Russian culture. When asked about that, Mrs. Mindlin related the concept to expectations in school:

> Much more in Russia; you can't even compare. First of all, homework—the kids have large homework assignments, which also have to be in correct format. (Parent interview, November 13)

As evidenced in these accounts, a cautious approach to life was characteristic of Yevgeny. When asked about his attitude toward taking risks, Mrs. Mindlin said that Yevgeny's preferred mode of interaction was to stay silent until he could say or do something perfectly, particularly if he had once made a mistake. This was also true in his venturing into English.

That her children learn English had been a very high priority for Mrs. Mindlin, as evidenced by the fact that on her own she had started teaching it to Yevgeny in Russia before they emigrated. She had written in her journal:

The first thing that Yevgeny told me this morning was, "Mom, I think I did a lot of stupid things with my English." My response to that was, "Like what?" It turned out that he did not say hello to his teacher when he saw her in the hallway. I also learned that when he did not understand something he would say to his teacher, "What?" I became so upset! (Parent journal, October 28)

At this interview, Mrs. Mindlin was asked what she thought was the most important factor in Yevgeny's ability to learn English. She responded that it was being in an environment where he was surrounded by English all of the time:

[W]here it comes at them from every direction: from signs, in school, from people talking, from television, from everywhere. ESL is probably not the most important factor, though it is important for them to go there because there is progress, thanks to ESL. It would have been great if they had had friends. (Parent interview, November 13)

She continued, however, saying that she really considered herself to be the biggest factor in the children's learning of English. She helped them with everything, although Yevgeny seemed to be getting along with less of her help now than before, except for science. An incident from her journal:

Yevgeny has so much homework that he hardly has any time to do it. Two days in a row we were memorizing English names of different worms. . . . Then we were hit by another problem: We had to prepare our own weather forecast and compare it with a phone service forecast. Both Yevgeny and I have a hard time understanding the forecast on the phone. The forecast is read with such speed . . . and all those miles and Fahrenheit . . . Until Yevgeny calculated that 21 miles per hour was only 9 meters per second, I felt that I was losing my mind. (Parent journal, November 11)

Listening skills are some of the first to be learned and practiced when learning a new language. Language learners practice with people (teachers, peers) as well as with tapes which have been made particularly for teaching listening skills. Often with these tapes, there is a visual cue—a workbook that puts the taped conversation into context. When learning a new language, using the telephone is one of the most difficult skills to master due to the lack of context or of visual cues. Listening on the telephone to prerecorded messages intended for native-language speakers incorporates decontextualization as well as rapidity of speech, with no chance to ask for repetition or a slower pace.

THE NEW UNIT ON WEATHER HAD BEEN USHERED IN BY THAT FINAL TEST ON THE pond creatures. This weather unit was taught by a student teacher and took place mid-November. She had wanted the desks rearranged in two concentric U shapes and had separated Lara from Yevgeny. On a particular day, the students were to carry out a project that involved comparing Fahrenheit and centigrade and making some predictions based on various circumstantial factors. The students were to work in groups of three. When those directions were given, Yevgeny seemed to be doing something else, so he was surprised when all of the children got up and rushed around to choose their groups. Carina immediately went to get Yevgeny, but by the time she got there, he had been placed with a couple of boys. When I asked Sheila if they had chosen him, she said that she noticed that they had needed a third person, so she had directed them to Yevgeny. Carina found another twosome to join. Out in the corridor, they were to sit in the sunshine with their thermometers and other equipment to record temperatures. One boy in Yevgeny's group seemed to take over; the other English-speaking student was told by Sheila to use the figures that the first one had written; Yevgeny did the same. His mother wrote her last entry in her journal the following day:

> Yevgeny feels very uncomfortable during science. Very often the students are assigned to work in groups of three, but Yevgeny usually does not get a group of his own. Instead, the teacher asks him to join an already formed group. So the only thing he has to do is to observe how others work. Yesterday these "others" definitely did something wrong during the experiment with temperature. Yevgeny noticed that the results of the experiment were "somewhat odd" but did not say anything and copied the results into his notebook. (The results were: 0° Fahrenheit in a warm and sunny room!) Now we have to use these "wonderful data" to make a diagram. (Parent journal, November 11)

This science unit was more language-based than the previous one had been. Students were asked to bring in reports from the newspaper, from television news, and from the weatherphone. They were also asked to make predictions and compare them with each other the following day in class. Some experiments were done by the students, but many times, the teacher did the experiment and the children watched. Much of what the student teacher discussed, she wrote on the blackboard for the students to copy into their notebooks, a strategy that was helpful for the cross-cultural students as well.

Science class even got into Yevgeny's wish list:

> I wish that: I could catch up with other students in science; this school to be a little more like my previous school; my family to be together; my classmates to speak Russian; my teacher to . . . (I don't know). (Student journal, November 17)

THE THIRD INTERVIEW WITH THE TEACHERS TOOK PLACE TWO MONTHS INTO THE school year. In answer to my request to tell about the previous two weeks, Sheila was most excited:

> Since we last met, some significant changes have happened. One is that the kids are including him now in their activities. The art teacher noticed that last time, also. They were all having a gay little time as they were cleaning up and getting ready to go home on Friday afternoon. Yevgeny and Evan were doing some sort of little dance, even. . . . It was the very same day that earlier he had (1) gotten 100 on his science test and (2) when I congratulated him, he had an enormous smile on his face, and I saw that same smile two hours later when I picked them up from art. The art teacher even said that he had been a different boy that day. I commented to someone else that I had gotten a smile out of Yevgeny that day and they said they had also. So, he woke up on the right side of bed or is finally feeling more comfortable. . . . I thought that smile was a breakthrough and the fact that he understood [that there would be a retest]. . . . I'm sure that it was not a big challenge; it was a very easy test, very easy test. To his credit, he picked up; he did what he was supposed to do. (Teacher interview, November 20)

Polly, the student teacher, who had joined us at lunch by this time added more:

> Earlier this week I asked him to hand out some of the booklets, the notebooks. And he said, "No, I don't know anybody's name." And so I said, "Well, you have to go around, then, and find out everybody's name." He said, "OK." And he went around and would say, "Are you Ben?. . ." and he did it. He did all I gave him. He came back and he smiled and sat down. (Teacher interview, November 20)

When asked if she had done this on purpose, Polly said that she definitely had. She had found that the students in class were making excuses for him, saying that he did not understand English, thereby getting him out of many assignments. She felt that there was some aspect of her assignments that the cross-cultural students would be able to do and should be expected to do.

> They have to know that they have to do it; that will make them more integrated into the classroom, I think, if they do everything that everyone else does.

Donna commented that he had smiled in her room before this particular breakthrough day. She was pleased with the progress that he was making in his ability to take math tests. She also commented that the other students were beginning to understand his strong math skills and to look to him for help in solving problems. In her class, she had felt that he had been engaged from the first day. The art teacher was also at this interview to give her perspective of what had happened that particular day in her class:

> He is very competent artistically. . . . The kids were talking last week, and they were saying, "I really feel sorry for him because he doesn't understand much English; it must be very hard for him." . . . And I said, "You know, the best way for a person to learn English a little better is for you to include him in your play as well as in your school." It was a small group; he wasn't even there then. When he came in, . . . they all descended on him; they were admiring him and tapping him on the shoulder and admiring his work. I could just see his little self-esteem rising. By the time the period ended, he was smiling. (Teacher interview, November 20)

I asked Yevgeny at our interview after this event what had happened that had produced such a change for him. His reply was that he had decided "to be more relaxed, to be more American." When asked if he could elaborate on that statement, he couldn't. He said simply that he had decided to relax. This transformation in attitude and demeanor had occurred at about the third month.

A MORE RELAXED ATTITUDE WAS EVIDENT DURING THE TWELFTH WEEK OF school, when I observed Polly's class right after snack time, which was just winding down when I came in. Yevgeny was at his desk munching on his last crumbs. Carina was at her desk, having finished. She immediately came over with the ruse of a specific question, and we chatted a bit. As our conversation was occurring, Yevgeny walked by slowly, then out into the hall. As soon as Carina started back to her desk, Yevgeny came by, and headed to his desk. He took a few steps past me, then shyly and slowly turned around, said "Hello," and continued to his desk.

By this time, the student teacher was handing out the science journals. She asked Yevgeny if he wanted to hand some out. He hesitated. She became distracted in another direction for a few seconds, but turned back and asked again if he wanted to. By this time, he had gotten halfway up out of his seat. He slowly took the journals and turned around to find their owners. When he got to the back row, students were happy to help him match journals with owners.

As the children were working in pairs on the science problem of the day, the student teacher worked with Yevgeny and his partner to help them arrive at the right answer.

Polly had some observations on her last day of student teaching:

We have played two "game shows" now . . . both were all science-oriented. He got one right . . . and he gave "high fives" to the other kids. That was the cutest thing . . . he was beaming, because he had done something right in the eyes of the other kids.

I try to treat them [cross-cultural students] like other kids. . . . I don't want to look over their shoulders, but I don't want to exclude them from anything they deserve either. I have spoken to them several times: You have to open your notebook, you have to take notes. Because if they don't do that, they'll just sit and daydream and won't concentrate. (Teacher interview, December 4)

Although daydreaming is not inconceivable for cross-cultural students, it is also important not to overgeneralize. These students had shown that they were very eager to integrate into the class as quickly as possible; they were highly motivated to do well. The stereotype needs to be broken apart; there may be factors other than daydreaming to be considered.

YEVGENY'S LAST INTERVIEW BEGAN WITH HIS LENGTHY EXPLANATION OF THE movie "Aladdin," which he had seen the previous weekend. He compared it with the story and movie in Russian and decided that this version was also completely different than the original story. He was fairly happy about his math test of the previous week, although he had not yet received the results. His response to *I Hate English* was that he could understand the girl's feelings:

I, too, hated English at first, but now I like it. At first I really hated it when my mom was teaching me in Russia. I thought I hated it because it was very hard. It is much more difficult to speak English than to understand English. That is why I am having problems. I understand much better than I speak. (Student interview, December 14)

During this interview, I asked Yevgeny what he felt was important in getting along with his classmates, other than knowing English:

Well, I haven't figured out the strategy yet; otherwise, I would have many more friends now. My problem is that I am too shy. And I can't change myself. (Student interview, December 14)

The next question concerned what people should do to be accepted by other people. His reply was that they should not be egocentric:

To get along, they have to give each other choices to play with and to listen to each other. (Student interview, December 14)

Friendships in the classroom was the major theme in the social adjustment of the students. With some of the students in this study, "buddies" or "friends" were assigned by the teacher to help acquaint them with the school. With the two cross-cultural students in this study who did have buddies, the attempt did not work. This is not to say that the buddy system does not work; it simply means that there may be more to establishing this relationship than first meets the eye. Indeed, a suggestion from one set of parents was to take the buddy system more seriously.

Making friends was an extremely important challenge for these cross-cultural students. However, Yevgeny's scholarly attitude impressed his teacher and peers as standoffish, or, in his teacher's terms, as "antisocial." Hence, the teacher and students did not respond warmly to him. Even though his studious approach to school and language gave him some satisfaction, he longed for an English-speaking friend, but did not know how to go about making one. His homeroom teacher had tried to have the boys in the class include him in their games, but that effort had petered out. Although some may consider it an imposition, it is important to find ways to enable shy students to make connections and, just as important, to encourage and teach their peers how to make others feel welcome.

As Yevgeny had been adjusting to school, Mrs. Mindlin had continued to work at her adjustment to life in the United States. At the final interview with her, she apologized that she had not had time to write in her journal. She was busy with two jobs: One was a volunteer job teaching English to newly arrived immigrant adults; the other, sponsored by the Russian families of Winsted, was teaching Russian to children whose families did not want them to lose their native language.

She felt that life had finally become a bit more routine in the previous month. The children were now able to do more and more on their own. She shared, with delight, an event in school that she felt was very important in Yevgeny's adjustment: He was sent with some other students, to help younger children use the jump ropes in gym. He was terribly proud that he could contribute, that he was the one who could explain something to someone else, that he could change roles for a while. She described much of the event in English, looking at me instead of the translator, to add weight to her words.

This point is extremely important for cross-cultural students. For much of their day, they are surrounded by language (and hence, activities) that is beyond them. Efforts are made, of course, to modify work so that they can do it, but there is little in their school lives that they can be proud of, that proves their competence to their peers, that boosts their self-esteem as they go about the job of acculturation. Hence, activities in which they can participate at the giving end instead of the receiving end—doing class chores, reading to or helping younger students, peer assistance—help not only their egos but also their classmates to accept them more easily as peers rather than pariahs.

While this event had been positive for Yevgeny, Mrs. Mindlin, personally, felt cut off from the school. She had not yet had an appointment with Yevgeny's teacher, although she realized that part of the fault was her reluctance to send back a form that asked her preferred time for a conference. She was not accustomed to being asked; she was accustomed to being told when to come in. She was confused that the school expected her to make a decision about which middle school Yevgeny should attend the following year; she felt she had no way to make that judgment. Although there was a plethora of information coming from the school about the PTA, she did not feel she was getting any information about the thing she wanted to know—the content of the curriculum. If, for example, the science notebook could have been brought home, she could have helped Yevgeny understand the concepts, so that he could have been better able to participate in class.

THE FINAL INTERVIEW WITH THE TEACHERS OCCURRED DURING THE FOURTEENTH WEEK of school, a few days before the winter break. Again, the interview started with the usual invitation to have the teachers talk about the past few weeks. Sheila was very excited:

> Yesterday was a momentous day; he came in bright and early at 8:30 and announced to me, "Today is my birthday, Mrs. Dinesen." Wooooh, I thought, whole sentence, big smile on his face. I have a kind of strange class, a motley group, very social, and unassuming. One of them came rushing up, in a caring kind of way, and said, "Yevgeny, it's your birthday, how wonderful!" Almost a second-grade kind of enthusiasm. . . . Lo and behold, at snack time he came out with two different assortments of cookies. . . . We sang to him, and apparently they sang to him in chorus. So he was beaming all day. It is nice to see that because there has been such growth. Usually you see them come along, but this is a kid who the first few weeks did not have a place; he was a loner. So I think he is feeling part of the group now. . . .[H]e came on as a little stranger, a little more of an "isolate" than the other kids. So if he had been with a different bunch of kids, this wouldn't have happened. Yesterday was his birthday, and the kids were so excited. That is unusual for fifth graders. (Teacher interview, December 16)

A week before that interview with the teachers, Yevgeny had made his last journal entry. The last cue for journal entries was to write a letter to a friend who was coming to the United States, telling him or her what was necessary to know about school in the United States. Yevgeny's letter:

Hi, Eugene:

American and Russian schools are so different! Nobody makes students do homework, but they do it anyway. And you don't have to address a teacher as if he is your commanding officer. The students regard the teacher as someone in between the friend and the parent.

And now about things that I study. Science is the most difficult class for me. During science we use microscopes, learn about different states of water at different temperatures, etc. Now we are studying rain forests. The most interesting thing is that we don't use textbooks and notebooks for science. The above things (textbooks and notebooks) we use only during math. And, by the way, my math notebook weighs at least half a kilogram, and the textbook is three times heavier.

By the way, we leave all our bags in the lockers outside the classroom. Inside we take only a textbook, a notebook and a binder. A binder has three metal rings that you can separate to put standard pieces of paper in. You also can put special pockets for your other papers. Well, I don't want to spend my whole letter on the description of a binder.

My favorite subject is ESL. ESL is an abbreviation for English as a Second Language. It is a program for immigrants. During ESL I work on the computer, listen to the tape recorder, and a lot of other things. Well, I think that's about it.

Goodbye, Yevgeny

Raina Popova

September 17: *I feel lonely in school because I don't know any English and I can't talk to the kids. Some of the kids are bad to me but some are nice. I have a friend in the other 6th grade. I play with her and we get along a little. Her name is Selma.*

And three months later:

December 8: *The last two days were like any others. Some of the kids were not nice to me. I could play only with Marsha because she is the only one to pay attention to me.* (Student journal)

Raina Popova and her four-year-old sister, Stefka, had arrived in July to join their father, who had been in the United States for almost two years, and their mother, who had preceded them by five months. In the intervening time, they had stayed with their grandmother in a small village near Sofia, Bulgaria. While their parents were still in Bulgaria, the family had lived in Sofia, but after the father's departure to find employment in the United States, the mother had moved back to her hometown. There had been great anticipation by the family about living in the United States. Raina felt that she had been envied by her friends in school; she was very excited to be coming to a "big, rich country, which it turned out to be" (Student interview, October 8). Raina was surprised by the size of buildings in the United States, and in early October couldn't seem to find anything she did not like.

Filled with high expectations early in September, Raina sat quietly listening to the conversation during the prestudy interview with her parents. Tall even for 11 years old, lanky, with short brown hair, sparkly eyes, and a warm smile, she could not understand this initial conversation in English, but watched carefully. Her little sister sat, coloring, on the floor of the small, minimally but comfortably furnished second-floor apartment. Mrs. Popova always offered the T/EI and me coffee and pastries during our interviews. Mr. Popov had lived close to work in a neighboring city when he had been here alone, but when his family joined him, they moved to this apartment because he had heard about the Winsted school system. Their apartment was over a reupholstering business on a busy street. Over them, on the third floor, lived a family whose daughter was in a different section of the same grade as Raina. A mechanical engineer, Mr. Popov had strong views about what was wrong with public schools in the United States; he had looked into sending his daughter to a private school, but had decided against it because the headmaster had talked so much about the students becoming "good persons"; Mr. Popov feared the school taught more than academics. He also articulated his concern about drugs in the public schools and was interested when I told him that the school was a participant in a program about drug resistance taught by the local police department. I shared with him my positive impressions of the teachers and the school, which I had seen for the first time earlier that day.

Mrs. Popova was an economist and understood some English, but realized that due to her lack of fluency and the differences in the economic systems of the two countries, she would not be able to find employment in her field. To prepare for that eventuality, prior to leaving Bulgaria she had taken some courses in hairdressing. She was continuing with her study of English and, having found out that the two countries have different licensing requirements for hairdressers, with more courses in that field. In the meantime, she was stuck in the consuming, eddying quagmire of simultaneously trying to find a job and daycare for her younger daughter. At the end of the interview, when I asked if there was anything about the school that I could explain to them, Mr. Popov replied that all they needed was a job for his wife.

Raina's eyes, smile, and demeanor were warm with those she knew, but she was shy with strangers. When we were at her home for subsequent interviews with her mother, Raina would participate appropriately, pleased to add her perspective to the issue being discussed. During her first interview at school, her eyes kept shifting back and forth from the T/EI to me, despite the fact that the translator was carrying the burden of the interview. When asked about that, the T/EI responded that Raina probably felt that she was being examined—the setting around a table with two adults might be reminiscent of an oral examination in Bulgaria—and that Raina wanted to see the reaction of both authority figures. In subsequent interviews, the setting was changed slightly and Raina also knew us better. An affirmative response from me to her queries about the date of an interview for herself or her mother often brought a shy smile.

Raina took my request about keeping a journal very seriously; she was the only student who wrote daily for the first two weeks of the study. Many of her entries were comparisons with what she was accustomed to in school in Bulgaria and her current feelings of isolation.

> Today our first class was reading. Everybody reads what they want. I'm reading a book in Bulgarian. We don't have a class like this in Bulgaria. After reading we had to have breakfast, but I couldn't have it because I had to study English in another room. The mathematics that I study in 6th grade I have already studied in Bulgaria in the 5th grade, so I find it very easy. Only it is hard to pronounce big numbers. It is surprising that here, in America, they don't have many textbooks whereas in Bulgaria we have 9 textbooks: in mathematics, history, geography, biology, literature, Russian, art, and music. . . . (Student journal, September 15)

> I cannot get used to this school yet because I cannot speak with the kids. Almost everybody laughs at me and speaks nonsense. I'd like very much to go back to Bulgaria because I can speak my language there and I have lots of girlfriends. I miss my school a lot. (Student journal, September 25)

Two of Raina's first impressions of the school were that it was not very tidy and the children were not very disciplined. She felt that students in Bulgaria had more respect for the teacher than the students in her present class had; despite the fact that the teachers showed them respect, she felt it was not reciprocated here. Other surprises she mentioned were the long earrings that girls wore to school, feet on the desks, loud talking, lack of oral examinations, and separate rooms for music and art. She enjoyed the cafeteria and recess.

> In Bulgaria we normally have five or six classes of 45 minutes each. After each class we have a five-minute break and after the third class we have a fifteen-minute break. Most schools have small stores (stands) for snacks. At noon some kids stay for lunch, others go home. Then some stay for the homework room where they do their homework and study for the following day.
>
> Once a week we have a "primary teacher" hour. In this class we do not study but we discuss different topics and we decide where to go all together—to the cinema, on an excursion, etc. (Student journal, October 27)

> In Bulgaria my school is not very big. It looks ugly on the outside but the inside is nice. I behaved like a student there. I did not put my feet up on

the desk; I did not talk in class, I did not wear long and polished nails. All students in the school behaved well. We had a different teacher for each subject. My class was very nice. We were the most outstanding class in the school. We were all good students. So was I. My favorite subject is biology, but unfortunately, we do not have it here. (Student journal, November 10)

RAINA WAS A SIXTH GRADER AT THE CARLYLE SCHOOL IN A WELL-ESTABLISHED, DIVERSE, heavily populated section of Winsted. Around the school, beautiful large homes with large yards are interspersed with well-maintained, more modest single-family homes as well as subsidized apartments for the elderly. A little farther away, duplexes, apartment houses, and large and small businesses crowd busy streets. The neighborhood used to be predominantly Greek. Now the Greeks here are into their second and third generations, and Hispanics and east Asians have moved into the neighborhood. This change is reflected in the school: A Spanish bilingual program has replaced the Greek one.

From the outside, the three-story brick school building looks like a Lego fantasy; in fact, the substantial additions made to the original gave the Carlyle School charm outside as well as inside. A multileveled interior gave most children welcome exercise, as they tromped up and down stairs to their various specialists. However, problems for the physically challenged became obvious when one child with an ambulatory problem hugged the inside wall so that other children could get by in their hurry. An adult who happened by slowed down to keep the boy company at his own pace. Brightly painted walls enliven the halls.

At the initial meeting with the ESL teacher on the third day of school, unpacked boxes lined the sides of her first-floor, large, centrally located room; only a few posters had been put up. This was due to the possibility that the room was going to be needed for a first-grade classroom. Two weeks into the school year, the move indeed was made to three small rooms on the third floor: one room that held two large tables and a desk, and two conference rooms that were large enough only for a table and four chairs each. Shelves crammed with books, kits, charts, and manipulatives lined the walls of all the rooms. Walls also were covered with posters where possible. One of the conference rooms also housed the copy machine for the teachers on that floor. That year, the population of the school was approximately 350, thirty-three percent of whom spoke a language other than English at home; there were about 60 students in the ESL program.

My interview with Lewellyn Carey, the principal, started with a question about the school's progress with "Core Values." The schools had been mandated the previous year by the administration to formulate a list of core values that would be similar to a "flag out in front of the school that portrayed what the school was all about." Although the parents and teachers had met separately and completed their individual lists the previous year, the limited job action had prevented further meetings to arrive at the shared list.

The limited job action was of great concern to Lew; he did not feel that the education of the children was being jeopardized in any way, but, as he saw it, there was a different attitude in the school. Morale was low among the teachers; workshops, in-service training, and faculty meetings had been affected by the teachers' absence.

From his perspective, the common goal of the teachers was "to provide service to the children" (Principal interview, November 23). This meant that teachers needed to respect the needs of the parents, and that each child's program might look very different from another's. Overall, academic achievement and respect for the family were the driving forces of education in Lew's school.

Asked about the impact of cultural diversity on the school community, he responded that he felt it was a "very healthy school; a very good introduction to the real world that these children are going to" (Principal interview, November 23). Lew explained that the high percentage of students who were bilingual was not typical of Winsted, but certainly of the world into which these children would enter as adults. In his eyes, the advantage was that the children would become bilingual; the problem was that it would not happen overnight. He stated that the solution required confidence by the teachers in the school system: Teachers would need to trust the total educational process—past, present, and future.

Responding to a query about how else he would like to characterize the school, Lew mentioned the school's involvement with the community: Parents were strongly urged to get involved early in their child's school experience; students were involved in appropriate civic activities such as recycling, singing at nursing homes, and a unit on gerontology that included an intergenerational pen-pal program between the fourth grade and members of the Senior Center, culminating in a luncheon attended by student, pen-pal, and student's parents. There was also a big emphasis on servicing children with any kind of special need in the mainstream classroom. He gave the example of the new class in the school that year, an integrated kindergarten of which eleven students had come from a mainstream nursery school and seven had come from the language development program. These children were taught by one teacher and two aides:

> [I]n this way, all students will receive a very good education and an early start on getting along with and respecting differences of different types of people. (Principal interview, November 23)

The school system of Winsted has been a leader in the concept of inclusion, and Lew Carey was a strong proponent of that concept.

THE CULTURE OF THE SCHOOL, AS FASHIONED PRIMARILY BY THE PRINCIPAL and secondarily by the teachers, was the first point of contact for all of these cross-cultural students and their families. Implicit or explicit, identified or not, the attitudes and behaviors of the school population, the assumptions and words that created meaning among members of the staff and students communicated the ethos that was the life of the school. Core values were the explicit lists of underlying beliefs in each school, which were generally similar from school to school. The cross-cultural students were not impacted by these lists of values except as they were played out by the members of the school culture. Although all of these values influenced the total culture of the school, the emphasis on the value of diversity, mentioned by all three schools, was particularly important for these students. For example, at the Brush Hill School, the emphasis on diversity was not simply relegated to a unit done in the third grade; there were reminders throughout the school of its importance and pervasiveness. The Svensens had been able to feel the warmth extended to them, in comparison with the disinterest that foreigners might feel in Norway.

In contrast, at the Valley School, the Torres' initial, positive impression was erased in a number of ways: The incident in which a school secretary walked away from Mr. Torres, even as he was speaking to her; the perception Mrs. Torres had of not being welcomed by the PTA or the teachers; and the sense that their daughter did not receive the help she needed contributed to a feeling hesitantly growing in the Torres family that there was a difference in the treatment of students from other cultures. For Mrs. Mindlin, contact with the school was minimal. The parents of each family seemed to be waiting for contact to be initiated by the teachers; undoubtedly, the teachers were waiting for the parents to initiate contact.

Here, at the Carlyle School, where 33 percent of the student body spoke a language other than English at home, the ESL room seemed to be the only spot where diversity was celebrated that year. Posters, signs, phrases, and flags decorated the hallway leading to the room. For the rest of the school, the International Night and mentoring of African American students constituted the nod to the rich multiculturalism within their ranks.

AT THE CARLYLE SCHOOL THERE WERE TWO SIXTH-GRADE TEACHERS WHO team-taught the two sections of the sixth grade. One teacher, Sarah Penzo, had the students for language arts and social studies; the other teacher, DebbieAnn Molinaro, was their math and science teacher. Both teachers had a homeroom section and worked on writing projects with those groups. Sarah was in her second year of teaching at this school; DebbieAnn had been in the system for four years. They discussed how I should identify myself if the occasion arose; it was decided that I should say that I was observing the whole class, not just Raina. They were very particular that she not be singled out in any way. The need to explain my presence never presented itself, nor did they introduce me to the class, which was the norm in this study.

Raina remembered her first day in school:

> When I came to school here, on the first day I did not speak with anyone because I did not know anyone. All the kids were talking about me and staring at me. On the second day, no one was paying any attention to me. I was feeling lonely. (Student journal, November 5)

Her homeroom teacher, DebbieAnn, remembered it differently:

> Her mother came in with her the first day and was going to stay with her all day. Poor Raina did not understand a word of anything anyone was saying to her; I gave her a journal just like I did to everyone else, and I asked her mother, to ask her to write an entry in Bulgarian. Her mother was not too thrilled about that and that bothered me; I felt that she [Raina] had pressure from her mother, and things weren't going to be learned the first day. The ESL teacher came in and talked with the mother, who finally left and Raina stayed the rest of the day. (Teacher interview, October 15)

Sarah Penzo's comment about the first day:

> She was very shy. She did not respond too much. What I am noticing now [three weeks later] is that if I come over to her and start talking to her and give her directions, she'll respond. (Teacher interview, October 8)

DebbieAnn Molinaro and Sarah Penzo were on the third floor of the newest addition to the Carlyle School. The two rooms were adjacent, and the teachers had strict rules for the flow of traffic when classes were changing. In DebbieAnn's room, the Reading Corner was inviting, with a couch, some large pillows, and a big sign that reminded everyone that there was no talking there. Posters about math, about the writing process, a world map with colored pins indicating newsworthy "hot spots" of the summer, a model of a family tree hinting at future class projects, blackboards, and shelves for storage lined the walls. For some unexpressed reason, Raina's name was frequently missing from the job list that one-half of the class did each week.

Sarah's room was similar in layout, although her emphasis was on her social studies corner with artifacts as examples for the unit on archaeology. Class rules were prominently displayed in both rooms and had to do with sequential talking, setting positive examples for the younger children, controlling actions and words, and helping others. Also, in both rooms were posters reminding the children of the motto learned in the "Efficacy Program": "Find Out How Good You Can Be." One day each week, students wore buttons that had "F O H G Y C B" written on them.

The extent of the ethnic diversity of the class was discovered when DebbieAnn did a lesson on emigration in December. Represented in class were heritages from Finland, Nicaragua, Russia, England, Ireland, Africa (with an explanation by DebbieAnn of the problem in using *Africa* as a designation instead of individual countries of Africa), France, Sweden, China, Bulgaria, Greece, Germany, Scotland, Argentina, Spain, Netherlands, Canada, and Italy. Some of these children had emigrated with their families; many were into the second or third generation in the United States. Some heritages had multiple members; many were represented by only one student. In an interview after this lesson, DebbieAnn commented on it:

> I think it was interesting for them [the students] to see that Raina was not the only person that does not share a heritage with other classmates; that Chris is the only person with a Chinese heritage, that Jaime is the only one with an Argentinean heritage. (Teacher interview, December 10)

THE FIRST DAY I OBSERVED RAINA WAS NEAR THE END OF THE FIRST WEEK OF SCHOOL. She was in social studies class with Sarah. Raina was in her seat in a group of five, sitting quietly during the class discussion of archaeology, paleontology, anthropology, and the like. Now and then she would lean over to the girl sitting next to her and make a comment; she initiated contact. As the children were rearranging themselves at the teacher's request for a different activity, some were flipping erasers. Raina tried quietly and gently flipping her pencil. The teacher explained the rules for the game of "Concentration," which was used to practice matching words and definitions. Raina participated as best she could; she understood what she was to do from watching others in her group, but was unable to read or understand any of the cards she was turning over. As luck would have it, she did not even get a 50 percent chance of choosing correct ones. However, at the end of the game, her body language did not indicate a disconsolate person; she gamely went back to her seat, ready for the next phase of class, which was going over the homework assignment for the next day.

The following day, in DebbieAnn's class, it was math time. Raina had the book open in front of her and alternated between looking at the book and at the teacher. She did not look frustrated, although her eyes wandered a little as though she were tired of concentrating so hard. This continued for approximately twenty minutes, at which point DebbieAnn asked the students to return to their original seats. The girl who had sat next to Raina in Sarah's room the previous day, Marsha, sat next to her again. The class, including Raina, copied the homework assignment from the board. Raina seemed to be asking Marsha a question; she made motions with her hands and said, "Many, many books." Marsha's brief comments in return did not seem to satisfy Raina, who tried again, with similar success.

In language arts the following day, Raina sat with a closed book in front of her while the teacher read the story to the class. Raina's demeanor indicated a more tired person; her eyes were downcast, wandering. It looked as though she were trying to force herself to listen now and then. After the reading, Ms. Penzo explained her expectations for homework; an example was written on the blackboard for all to copy into their notebooks so that they would have a model to follow. As the class was doing this, Sarah came to where I was standing and shared her concern that she really did not know what to do with Raina during this time; it seemed so wasted. Should she copy the model from the board or word meanings from a dictionary? During the conversation, Raina had decided that she should copy the model from the board and started to do so. At this point, the ESL teacher came to pick up Raina for her English lesson.

As can be seen from these examples, Raina was trying very hard to integrate into her classes as best she could: She imitated behavior; she initiated contact; she participated in activities she could not totally understand; she tried to follow. Each of her attempts these first few days seemed to meet with at least indifference and apathy, and in some later situations, downright hostility.

THE ISSUE OF FRIENDSHIP AND PEER RELATIONSHIPS WAS A VERY DIFFICULT AND painful one for Raina. Accustomed to having many friends in Bulgaria, she was having a very difficult time making any friends here. The issue came up constantly in her journal entries and in her interviews. She felt the reason was her inability in English:

> Nothing special happened today. As usual, I did not play with many kids because I cannot talk to them and they avoid me. I play with Marsha and Selma only. (Student journal, October 20)

During her first interview, she told of two separate incidents that had happened in the first few weeks of school. The first incident had happened during a time when I was in the classroom.

> The kids are hostile to me, they avoid me, they make fun of me. [When asked for an example, she said] Everyone in the class was numbering off to be in a group. I heard "4" before me, so I answered "5." Everyone

laughed; I did not understand that we were to go only to 4. (Student interview, October 8)

The other incident had happened earlier in the week:

> In music class, the teacher was seating us in assigned places. She told me to sit in a particular seat. I went to sit there and the girl told me that she did not want me to sit there, even though the teacher had said to. I got up and moved to another seat. (Student interview, October 8)

When pushed by the T/EI that perhaps she did not understand them, Raina replied that there was no mistaking that the student said that Raina was not to sit in the empty chair. In the counting-off incident I had observed, Mrs. Molinaro had been very quick to reprimand the students for their laughter.

Raina's relationship with her peer, Marsha, intrigued me. They sat together in DebbieAnn's class, but they did not walk to the cafeteria or to specialists or to special events, nor did they change classes together. They arrived and left the cafeteria separately, but they ate lunch next to each other and were together at lunch recess. Marsha did not seem to have a different set of friends she socialized with; she was a loner. This relationship was explored with both Raina and the teacher. I asked Raina how it was that she was able to find Marsha as a friend. She replied

> I watched Marsha on the playground and found that she seemed particularly helpful and kind to Selma so I picked her for a friend. (Student interview, October 8)

I continued with a question as to whether it would have been easier for her if Ms. Molinaro had picked someone to be her friend for the first few weeks, even if it had later turned out that the friendship did not "go anywhere." Raina said that it would have been infinitely easier for her. A few days later, Mrs. Molinaro had a very different perspective on this same topic:

> I paired the two up [Raina and Marsha] on the first day of school. That was why I had them sitting next to each other from the beginning of the year. I did it because Marsha is a very laidback, sort of slow-moving person; she is a very intelligent girl, but physically she just sort of lumbers along. But she has such a sweet nature, and she is very patient. So I knew that she would not turn around and attack Raina like, "Come on, let's go, you should have known that."
>
> JBC: I have noticed that the interaction between them is usually initiated by Raina and not by Marsha. I was wondering whether that was getting to be too heavy a burden for Marsha.

DebbieAnn: I don't think so. I think Marsha doesn't think to do it.
(Teacher interview, October 15)

Somehow, Raina did not even know that a "friend" had been assigned to her. She felt totally abandoned, having to find her own way, as expressed poignantly and repeatedly in her journal entries. Despite the fact that Marsha sat next to Raina in all of DebbieAnn's classes, I did not see Marsha once lean over to initiate help for Raina. She answered if Raina asked, but otherwise did nothing for her. One of the times that this was most obvious was during the DARE program toward the end of the first month of school. A police officer came into the classroom to talk with the students about drug resistance. Raina played with her DARE folder, a ruler, her pencil. The officer wrote something on the board and asked the students to copy the word and its definition into their folders. Raina realized that the children were writing in their folders, but was unable to find the correct page to write on. No one leaned over to help her identify on which page she was to write. Just when she finally found the correct page by looking at her neighbors and started writing the definition, the officer erased the blackboard. Raina closed her folder; her whole body sagged. She had looked over in my direction fairly often that day. One of the times, she looked very angry: Her eyes were dark, her brow furrowed. She desperately wanted help, but I had been told not to single her out. When we later talked about this incident during an interview, her feeling was that at this point, she wanted to understand and participate more than anything; being singled out for help would have been welcomed.

Three days later, in language arts again, Raina was sitting at her desk with her head in her arms when I came in at 9:00 AM. The class was working on a project to celebrate their having finished a book; they were making mobiles. Raina had not read it, but in an effort to integrate her into the project, Sarah had decided that Raina could make a drawing that would be incorporated into a mobile. Sarah gave her the book and the special paper and showed her what to do. Raina seemed to understand what to do and went to work.

About 25 minutes into class, the announcement came over the loudspeaker that the sixth graders were to proceed to the "bus evacuation" practice. Raina saw everyone getting up; she did not. Eventually everyone lined up to go out and Raina decided that she should put away her things. No one, including Marsha, stopped by her desk or spoke to her in any way. As the students were lining up, Ms. Penzo reminded them that they were to be models for the first-graders and were to explain to them what procedures were used for bus evacuation. The sixth-graders had done this procedure for six years and were to pass on their knowledge; furthermore, they were to behave properly. Ms. Penzo led the line down the stairs. Seeing the teacher walking out the door with the students, Raina decided that she too should line up and was the very last in line. Marsha had not ignored her to be with friends; she was alone, too, in the middle of the line. Walking down the stairs with Raina, I tried to briefly and simply explain what was happening and what she might need to do. She nodded that she understood and explained that she was a "walker." Once outside at the bus, the sixth-graders were paired up with first-graders and told to get on at the front door of the bus and off at the rear exit. The second time around, the principal had them sit down, closed the doors, and asked the sixth-graders to explain the procedure to the first-graders. As I left, I heard Lew asking the boy sitting across from Raina to explain to Raina's first-grader what was happening.

DECIDING TO FOLLOW UP THE INCIDENT DURING CHORUS, I GOT TO CLASS a little early so that I might discover the chorus/music teacher's perception of Raina. Because I had promised Raina confidentiality, I phrased the question as, "How has it been for Raina? Have there been any special incidents that stand out?" The music teacher was quite aloof; she said that Raina was a quiet and shy girl who did not know much English, but that she didn't see any reason why Raina should not be in chorus. Before I could pursue the question further, the teacher frantically turned to the topic of her accompanist, who had not yet arrived. Soon thereafter the accompanist came, and so did the students.

I continued to observe Raina with the other specialists: physical education, art, music, and ESL. She did not attend the library period with her class. In physical education, lacrosse was introduced the day I was there. Raina was sitting near Marsha, but there was no exchange between them. After some instruction, the children were to pair up—one boy and one girl—to practice throwing and catching the ball. Raina had a very difficult time picking a boy. She felt very uncomfortable: She looked down, she let time slip by, she did not choose. Finally, with slight impatience in her voice, the teacher paired her with Boris, a student with a Russian background. Once that was done, Raina participated fully and seemed to have fun. A free and easy interaction between genders can cause great concern for some cross-cultural students. It was likely that Raina's shy personality made it difficult for her to pick a boy. Perhaps Raina was accustomed to being told, not being asked, whom she would like for a partner, even one of the same gender.

When the students were invited by the art teacher into the art room, the students went to assigned seats. There didn't seem to be a place for Raina; the art teacher asked a boy to give up his seat and get another stool for himself. Nor did Raina have a folder, as many others seemed to have. Because Raina had not understood the teacher's directions about what materials to gather, I took her over to the table of materials and tried to explain the project to her. The art teacher soon joined us and reiterated what I had said. At a time when the art teacher asked the students to come around the table where they were to watch a procedure, Raina again did not go until I motioned that she should be there; nor did she follow the simple, clear instructions to put away equipment at the end of the period.

This incident made me curious about the perception of Raina by her mainstream teacher near the end of her first month. For DebbieAnn, a teacher for four years, Raina was the first student she had had who knew no English at all. She had had other bicultural children in her classes, but they had picked up some English before entering her class. DebbieAnn was most enthusiastic in her assessment of Raina's first month in school:

> Actually I was quite impressed with the other kids in my class in that they were somewhat friendly. Someone asked her if she wanted to go to lunch the second day of school and walked down with her. Unfortunately, they have not continued to be as consistent.
>
> She [Raina] herself has shown amazing growth in terms of language. We went from the very basics of hello and goodbye to her showing me what she has done, which is usually math. The spelling is obviously not in question, nor the writing; so she'll show me her math when she gets squared away. When we are writing in journals, she'll write sometimes, but I don't think she likes to. I think she is feeling some pressure to write only in English. So she'll most often opt to read silently. Or, I have told her she can do her ESL work then, too. (Teacher interview, October 15)

DebbieAnn also spoke of the longer phrases that Raina used when asking to be excused to go to ESL and about the fact that the previous day Raina had actually understood some directions that DebbieAnn had given and had followed them, instead of following her classmates' actions. DebbieAnn had commented to Raina, "You understood!" to which Raina had smiled.

> That is the other thing I am seeing a lot of—the smiles. It was a very dead-pan face for a while. . . . I know the insecure feeling you have [speaking a foreign language]. (Teacher interview, October 15)

Working with the computer was part of bonus time on Fridays: If students had all their work done, they had options for a 45-minute period at the end of the week. Raina never had homework to catch up on and had gone to the computer lab a few times. The previous Friday, it had been DebbieAnn's turn to supervise the computer time. She described how she had been impressed with Raina's quick understanding of the procedure, once it was explained. Raina had been unable to read the directions on the screen, but once DebbieAnn explained them, Raina was fine.

Curious about the impact on their teaching styles, I asked if having students from other cultures had made a difference; Sarah answered,

> That's hard to answer because I feel that I am still developing my style. I realize that I definitely need to pay more attention to students who have different needs from the average student and how to accommodate those needs. . . . I feel that I need to be more organized in the way I present things . . . and that I need to call her back the next day and say, "I didn't receive what you were working on." I don't know that it is changing my style as much as it is changing the way I organize my day and my work. . . . Basically everyone in my class is to be treated the same way; everyone gets the same respect, the same attention from me. However, kids will get maybe more or less attention, depending on their need. (Teacher interview, October 8)

DebbieAnn did not feel that having a cross-cultural student in her class had actually modified her overall teaching style. She also felt that she was still perfecting her style. She often found that she proceeded and then backed up with the few students who needed extra help. In answer to the question as to whether she found herself treating Raina differently from the other students, she said,

> [O]ne on one, personally, no. I treat her just like any other sixth grader. Yes, I probably do treat her differently in the sense that I maybe monitor more closely if she is paying attention, if she is writing what is on the board. . . . But I have to say that she makes more of an effort than a lot of the kids. Like in the morning, she comes over to me and says, "Good morning"; and in the afternoon, she makes it a point to say, "Goodbye." (Teacher interview, October 15)

THE CLASSROOM STRATEGIES OF THE FIVE TEACHERS WHO TOOK PART IN THIS STUDY ranged on a continuum from egalitarian to integrative. While no teacher was strictly at one end of the continuum or the other, there seemed to be tendencies toward particular strategies. Egalitarian strategies grew out of a strong commitment to treating all students equally. This meant that students were not to be singled out; the teachers implied that focusing on a student accentuated the problems the student might have. It was better that the student find her or his own way initially, but they were always welcome to ask the teacher for help. This egalitarian strategy was difficult for these cross-cultural students because they were accustomed to being top students without asking for help. The teachers using this approach did so not only out of a commitment to equality in the classroom and to the discovery approach to teaching, but also, perhaps, because of their commitment to the individual. That is, they were working out of a cultural value of individualism, allowing the students to work things out as they wanted to or as they were able to. Also at work were unconscious expectations of how native-born children of the same age act or what they want. The strong emphasis by these teachers on the autonomy of the individual exhibited itself in different ways: Guiding the cross-cultural student to participate in class activities was not used immediately—for example, job assignments were either left to student initiative or were minimal, and students were expected to approach the teacher if they needed help. Reshaping or adjusting the material to fit the student's ability or finding similar material at an easier linguistic level was minimal. DebbieAnn Molinaro felt that any extra attention would bring loud complaints from the other students that one person was getting more attention than another in a classroom, where being fair was a very high priority.

At the other end of the continuum, integrative strategies were those that tried to make the child feel a part of the class as quickly as possible: having the student participate (even without language) in as many activities as possible, making the student part of the job rotation immediately, identifying a desk group by the cross-cultural student's name, giving the student extra attention in class to help the student follow, finding material that the student could work on when the rest of the class was doing something above his or her linguistic ability.

These widely differing strategies on the egalitarian–integrative continuum meant different amounts of involvement with the cross-cultural students. For these students, there is often, at first, a need for more guidance than we might give similar native-born agemates. Guided participation (Rogoff, 1984) provides a bridge between old and new information, enabling the student to take a step that is slightly challenging, but that is within range with adult assistance. The teacher's role is to provide support that is adjustable and temporary (Gavelek, 1984) as the management of the problem is transferred fully to the student. The more this can be accomplished in the mainstream classroom, the easier the adjustment will be for both the teacher and the cross-cultural student.

ASKED IF THERE WAS ANYTHING THAT STOOD OUT IN HER MIND THAT HAD BEEN a particular problem for Raina, DebbieAnn said,

> I find myself focusing so much on the social part of it, but I think in the
> sixth grade that is so much of everyday life. The other day I was coming

out of class to go get my own lunch, and I came down the stairs and saw her. At the bottom of the stairs, I heard two male voices saying "Raina,na,na,na. . . ." They disappeared around the corner. I looked at Raina and asked her if she was OK and she sort of nodded. I told her to go ahead to lunch, and I followed behind her. I went into the cafeteria; I couldn't identify the boys, although they were obviously from my room.

So when they came back up from lunch, I just said to the class very briefly and quickly, "When you come into a new school, as a student, . . . it is very, very difficult to fit in with people. . . . It is very important to treat everyone in your class with respect. I'm not asking you to be best friends with everyone, but I am asking you to treat everyone the same and to treat everyone respectfully. That means I don't want to hear anyone being called names, and I don't want to see people by themselves." (Teacher interview, October 15)

A question about Raina's impact on the class brought out an important perspective:

Yes, I do [think she has had an impact on the class] in a small sense. I think it is hard to judge at this point, a month into school. . . . We did talk [about Bulgaria] the first day. The sad thing . . . is that the only map we have is at the back of the room. . . .

I don't like to single out; obviously you are not saying to single someone out, but I don't like to single someone out and talk about it much because then, I think *fair* is the big word in the sixth grade, and it gets to be, "How come you are always talking about her. . . ." Also, not to make the person who is new in the class feel like [he or she is] the focus of what is going on. . . . I think the impact she has had is . . . others' taking the initiative to help her, to give her guidance in what to do, to open up the social circle. (Teacher interview, October 15)

One further perspective from this interview dealt with peer relationships as DebbieAnn saw them at this point.

In terms of [asking people to help], I haven't stressed that too much. . . . I was always brought up that if you wrong someone else, if someone else tells you to apologize, it is a meaningless apology. So I think that I go with that with the help, too. . . . [T]he thing I have to monitor is the giggling, the snickering, whatever. That has toned down tremendously, but the first couple of times it happened, I addressed it immediately. Those kinds of things, I don't let go. This is a class that readily attacks. (Teacher interview, October 15)

During the interview at home, when Raina's mother was asked what kinds of issues had arisen in Raina's first month in school, she started with an example of academic work: Raina was having problems not with the material to be learned, but with mathematical conventions; that is, conventions that were different here in the United States from those in Bulgaria. She then moved on to the social aspects: that children made fun of Raina for not knowing the language and for not knowing computers. No one had shown her anything about the computer games until the teacher finally took some time with her and pointed out key phrases. Mrs. Popova stated that language had been the most basic factor for the adjustment of the whole family; she could not conceive of life without fluency in language. Raina seemed to be picking up chunks rather than single words. However, one month into the school term, Mrs. Popova felt that for a shy person who is not comfortable in all situations, Raina was adjusting well; that she was more comfortable in math than she had been.

Mrs. Popova, herself, had been a little disappointed in their time in the United States. She and her husband had had high expectations of a good business prospect from a relative who lived in Vancouver. That had not worked out at all, so her husband had moved to the east coast, where they did not have any relatives. Her husband felt that the first company with which he had worked on the east coast was filled with incompetent people. He had moved on to another run by a compatriot. Mrs. Popova could not say what specifically disappointed her; she thought it was perhaps the lack of English and friends other than Bulgarian ones. In addition, she felt tied to the apartment because there was no day care for her youngest. She had found that most of her USAmerican contacts had been very friendly and patient with her attempts in English; however, she felt that the friendships were very superficial.

IT WAS THE MIDDLE OF THE SECOND MONTH WHEN I OBSERVED RAINA IN music and chorus again. In chorus, which consisted of 100 students from the fourth- fifth- and sixth-grade classes, classroom teachers helped maintain discipline. Raina stood between two girls who were in her class. There seemed to be no interaction that I could see between the girls, so I was surprised when one of the girls was called out of the room by one of the teachers. When the teacher came back, she whispered to me that there had been some foot stomping in that row. The teacher said that it must have been accidental and had asked this particular girl to watch over Raina. There was no difference in the behavior of the girl after the request by the teacher.

The ESL observation was preceded by an interview with the ESL teachers, Tanya and Rod. Their perceptions of Raina:

Rod: Right from the outset, I have thought of her as a very, very easy-going, a very pleasant girl, eager to want to work, to want to learn. She consistently gets her work done; . . . I think she is making very good progress. She is very pleasant to work with.

Tanya: I think in the beginning she was a little frightened. When I asked her mother to leave that first day, I think she was unhappy. I think she felt deserted, and I think she wanted me to fix it somehow. . . . After a couple of days, I think she felt more at ease because she knew the routines and understood the expectations. . . .

Rod: [She is] certainly very much at ease here in ESL. She is very comfortable here. (ESL Teacher interview, October 20)

When Raina came in for ESL class, she and Rod greeted each other in a casual, friendly fashion. During class, there was a lot of positive emotional response from Raina: smiles, clapping, pretend-groaning. It was clear that she did, indeed, feel very comfortable in this setting. Rod was full of compliments and encouragement. She had class alone with Rod for a half-hour and then was joined by another student who had been in the United States for one year, but still needed a lot of support in English. In here, also, I found Raina watching me; her body language indicated that she seemed pleased to be in a situation where I could see how well she could do. She groaned audibly when told she had only ten more minutes. She was very relaxed in this class, eager to do her work, to communicate, to show her knowledge. When told that they could take out their mid-morning snacks to eat while they continued the lesson, she asked, "Which is correct: 'May I get my snack?' or 'Can I get my snack?'" When Rod answered that *may* was really more correct, she beamed, "I said, *may;* Ilya [the other ESL student] said, *can!*"

Raina was asked her reactions to these classes. She agreed that she was doing better in English; that everything seemed easy in art, music, and gym. Her responses that day to my questions were one sentence answers, for example, "I like going to them, to do all those things." When asked why she thought that they were easier than the other classes, she responded, "They are like a diversion; they are relaxing" (Student interview, November 18). ESL was her favorite class; when asked what was best and worst about it, she replied that best was the type of homework she was assigned and the teacher; there was no worst part at all. She felt that she was really learning something. When pushed why this was, she responded,

Mr. Rod speaks more to me and I remember more. (Student interview, November 18)

I also observed Raina at lunch. She did not walk down the three flights of stairs to lunch with anyone, but after she had gotten her food, she went to her usual place with Marsha and Selma. When asked how it was that she knew what to do, she said that her upstairs neighbor had told her a little before the beginning of school, and then she had just observed. The threesome that sat together did not talk to each other; nor did they wait for each other to finish. That particular day, as Raina was leaving, a girl from Sarah Penzo's class came up to her and said, "Where'd you buy your sweatshirt?" Raina looked at her blankly. The girl repeated it, and when Raina still looked blank, the girl went off in a huff. Rachel, a classmate of Raina's yelled over, "You know, sweater, shirt . . . (fingering her own). . . Where'd you get it?" Raina still looked blank. I tried, and finally it was established that it came from Boston. Once out on the playground, except for one time when there was a game that involved about ten students, the three wandered around aimlessly, not very enthusiastic about anything they were doing.

DURING THE SEVENTH WEEK OF SCHOOL, WHEN I WALKED IN TO MATH CLASS, the students were working in groups, but Raina was alone. DebbieAnn immediately came over to say that the work on estimation involved so much language that she had given Raina different work to do. Speaking deliberately and looking at Raina, she continued, "but many teachers and I agree that Raina probably follows directions better than the English speakers." She gave Raina a pat on the back and left. As she was leaving, Raina gave me a blank look and then shrugged her shoulders. I asked her if she had understood; she said no. When I simplified the language to say that Mrs. Molinaro thought she was a good student, Raina gave a little smile and settled into the worksheet that she had been assigned.

Later that week, when I arrived it was not yet time for math, and the students were working on a variety of lessons, Raina was playing with a Rubic cube. She continued to play with it for about twenty minutes until math started. The math lesson was on exponents. DebbieAnn asked Raina if she had studied exponents in Bulgaria; Raina did not answer. The question was repeated; still no answer was forthcoming. It was only as the teacher was doing the calculations on the board that Raina was able to participate. Indeed, in the ensuing problems, she was able to contribute two answers: One was incorrect because she had not understood how exponents worked, but the other was correct. Her happiness to be a part of the class, to have contributed a correct answer, was palpable.

IN WRITING CLASS, THE STUDENTS WERE CONTINUING THEIR AUTOBIOGRAPHIES, which would be written over the course of the school year. The first topic apparently had been something about the day they were born. They had been asked to bring in baby pictures, which were displayed on a bulletin board. Raina's was not there. The current chapter was to describe their first day in kindergarten. Some had finished, and in order to inspire others, DebbieAnn had two students read their chapters out loud to the class. After the stories were read, the children were to get in pairs for critiquing purposes; DebbieAnn told Raina she could work on ESL homework. I asked DebbieAnn if I might work with Raina on her autobiography instead. She could write it in Bulgarian; possibly the translator could translate it, and then hers also could be hung with the rest on the bulletin board, but in both Bulgarian and English. DebbieAnn shrugged her shoulders and said, "Why not?"

After some explanation, Raina started on this project. I wrote a brief note to her mother, explaining the project, and included some questions Raina needed answered about the topic. As I left, Raina was busy writing; I went to speak briefly to DebbieAnn, who greeted me with, "Were you able to get through to her? Didn't she scowl at you?" Evidently, for DebbieAnn, Raina's smiles of the first month had now been replaced by constant scowls and blank stares.

The next time I saw Raina, she was on the couch in the Reading Corner. She had just returned from ESL and was waiting for her class to return from social studies. I mouthed, "Hello"; she made no response. Three attempts later, she responded slightly. We sat there and quietly chatted; she initiated a question about her interview that afternoon. At the class changeover time, DebbieAnn came over and told me in a most exasperated way about her recent exchange with Raina. The day after I had worked with Raina on the writing, DebbieAnn had asked to see it when Raina arrived the next morning. Raina looked blank, so DebbieAnn took her over to the table where we had sat and she pantomimed sitting and writing. Still Raina looked blank. DebbieAnn gave up in total frustration.

There were other events that were happening that might have added to Raina's discomfort. At about the same time, I got a call from the T/EI relating a plea from Mrs. Popova who had asked for the T/EI's insight as to how to handle a situation. There had been a birthday party going on in the upstairs apartment for the neighbor child who was in the other section of the sixth grade. Raina had not been invited but had run into all her classmates who were going to it. Visually reminded of her rejection, she had sobbed at length. Her mother wondered if there were some way in which she could or should enlist the help of the teacher.

At the interview after this event, Raina was shown the SSPS pictures. Her responses were slow and sparse. The first picture was of the classroom and teacher:

> The child has just taken a math test. She is happy. She will go home and make the mother happy. (Student interview, November 6)

The second picture, of the playground, brought a little more description:

> The kids are playing ball. She is watching them play. . . .They told her they do not want her to play. She seems very sad. She doesn't know why they don't want her to play with them. She might have bumped into a kid, or made the kid fall, and that is why they don't want her to play with them. They might get to be friends in the end. (Student interview, November 6)

With the third picture, Raina had to be assured, once again, that there was not a right or wrong answer. The story could be whatever she wanted it to be. This picture was of the parents and child in an office:

> The girl goes somewhere with her mother and father. . . . They talked to the teacher and he said that she was doing well. . . . She had gotten a sheet of paper to take home to her parents. . . . The girl is feeling happy; she'll get good marks; she'll do well. (Student interview, November 6)

The fourth and final picture showed a student studying, two books to one side, an open book, paper, and pencil in front of her:

> She doesn't know what to write about. She's thinking about it. She feels sad because she expects a bad mark . . . . The subject is writing . . . She won't get a good mark . . . because she doesn't know what to write. (Student interview November 6)

During this interview, I asked Raina about an incident Sarah Penzo had related to me during her interview three days earlier. As part of the unit on archaeology, Sarah had organized a "dig" in the play area of the school. Sarah had given her perspective on the event:

> I don't know if it is depression; that is what it looks like to me. She seems very, very, very apathetic about everything. Not just schoolwork, like: I don't want to do school work. It seems to be anything—holding up a map in class. . . . She took part in the archaeological dig yesterday morning. I mean, that is definitely different, something that is not done every day, something that seems exciting even if you did not understand the lan-

guage—like, why are these people digging in the sand. And she . . . I had told her she needed her coat, she went out without it; she came back in to get it and Rod [the ESL teacher] came out with her. He said that she was looking so depressed that he decided that he would come out with her to be with her group. That was helpful because it meant an extra pair of hands for me. She finally, slowly got into it. (Teacher interview, November 3)

Asked three days later to tell me about the "dig" in Ms. Penzo's class, Raina had this to say about it:

Raina: Not very interesting.

JBC: What would have made it more interesting?

Raina: If they had gone on a field trip. In Bulgaria they took field trips, to see things. They would go out for walks, but not to excavations. (Student interview, November 6)

The transition from book learning to experiential learning, from a transmission model to a discovery model, was another challenge for all of these students. Most made the adjustment with eagerness, except when it jeopardized the student's image of self as a good student. Raina's image of herself as a very good student had been obvious from the start. She had commented early in the school year about some of the differences in the lessons; she missed studying history, geography, biology, and literature. This day I discovered that the breadth and variety of subjects in sixth grade in the United States had eluded her; she was surprised to find that bridge-building was a part of science. Her response:

In Bulgaria they do the building of bridges in arts and crafts, like candle holders and other things. (Student interview, November 18)

DebbieAnn commented on Raina's participation in the "Bridge" project in science; she was the "carpenter" in the group of four students. DebbieAnn felt that the others in the group had been incredibly patient with Raina, but that even to them, she gave no response but a confused, blank look. DebbieAnn found it hard to believe since she knew that Raina was a bright student. She commented,

I think that the only thing that I am feeling concerned about at this point is . . . about her not engaging more with the kids. I feel like the kids have tried to be very positive towards her. Last week I spoke to some girls who . . . that day said, "Do you want to eat with us?" and she sort of looked at them. They repeated it many times; finally I said, "Raina, they are asking

if you will eat lunch. Go downstairs with them." She didn't answer anyone, but at least kind of acknowledged what was being said. So, the following week I asked the girls again, and they said that they would offer,
but that she did not eat with them. (Teacher interview, November 3)

DebbieAnn did go on, however, to talk about how Raina was a little
more responsive when she was in a one-to-one relationship, when she did
not have to pick out a word here and there in a general lecture.

When I do have time to sit just with her, she is very responsive. A few
times recently when I felt she was more in with the class, I have students
sit with her. She had some trouble with an ESL assignment one day, and
she came over and asked for help. I was in the middle of . . . something
else, so I asked a couple of girls to go over and help her. That seemed to
work out nicely. There was much more emotion there; there was smil-
ing. Maybe she is just not a risk-taker. (Teacher interview, November 3)

The personal priorities or the individual uniqueness of these cross-cultural students naturally had an impact on the way in which they dealt with the
challenges of their adjustment. As with children anywhere, for some, finding a
social base has to be accomplished before learning can take place; for others,
the first option is to please the teacher (Almy and Genishi, 1979). For Raina, a
variety of friends was the elusive grail. During the fourth week of school, she
could talk about the two friends who were nice to her and with whom she got
along, although from an observer's perspective, the friendships seemed very
thin. She was unable to break into the closed circles of friendships in the sixth-
grade classroom, and the infrequent advances from her classmates were not
reciprocated by her. She seemed unable to make friends with anyone beyond
the two; even at the end of the study, she bemoaned the fact that she did not
seem to be able to play with all her classmates. This inability (hers and her
peers') and the subsequent isolation became very painful for her and affected
her relationships, her outlook on the rest of her experience, and her ability to
deal with the challenges of the adjustment. "If only I could talk to the kids" was
a comment heard more than once from her. She was a serious student, but
friendship was also very important to her. Both of these priorities could be
seen as she tried to make sense of the classroom instruction in those first few
weeks, and also as she tried to make friends with the students in the class. Neither strategy worked. The only bright spot in the day was the time spent in ESL
where she felt valued and able. Because she had some control over her performance there, she poured her energies into that academic pursuit, hoping that
friendships would develop as language ability increased.

THE TOPIC OF PEER RELATIONSHIPS WAS EXPLORED EXTENSIVELY WITH RAINA'S homeroom teacher. In early October, DebbieAnn had felt that her students had been very open and receptive to Raina. She told of an incident the students had related to her in which they tried to ask Raina to play at recess and even got a Russian-speaking student to translate (Raina had studied Russian in Bulgaria), but that she simply continued to draw in the sand with her foot. DebbieAnn continued,

> They came to me concerned because they said that she didn't understand what they were saying . . . so I don't know if she really didn't understand or if she wanted to sort'a hang back and observe for a while. That would be a natural reaction from kids: "Hey, we tried." (Teacher interview, October 15)

In early November, during an observation, DebbieAnn reported that Mrs. Popova had come in to talk about the hard time Raina was having. So DebbieAnn and the class had had a discussion about how one goes about treating those who are new to the country. DebbieAnn then said that afterward, she counted nine people who had said goodbye to Raina that afternoon, to which Raina did not reply once.

There had been another incident in early November, which, with the mother's permission, I related to DebbieAnn. At snack time, Raina had taken out her snack of a sandwich and a small box of juice. She felt that all the children in her desk group pointed at it and talked and laughed about it. Her mother said that Raina refused to take that size juice box and a sandwich anymore. When DebbieAnn explored the incident with Raina's groupmates, they did admit that something had been said that, if one did not know the language, could have been interpreted as ridicule. DebbieAnn had taken the opportunity to talk to the students about how important body language and tone of voice are when the language is foreign.

The relationships within the class are dependent on the members of the class, on the tone that the teacher sets, and on the response of the cross-cultural student. It is important here to take into consideration the teachers' concerns about the psychological makeup of fifth- and sixth-graders and the impact that might have on accepting others. In the previous chapter, Sheila Dinesen had commented about Yevgeny and Carina's class:

> I have kind of a strange class, a motley group . . . They are very young, very social. . . . That is unusual for fifth-graders. If he [Yevgeny] had been with a different bunch of kids, this [their joyful greeting on his birthday in December] would not have all happened. (Teacher interview, December 16)

DebbieAnn commented on the social nature of Raina's class:

> I find myself focusing so much on the social part of it, but I think in
> sixth grade that is so much of everyday life.... There's a lot of social dis-
> cussion, a lot of emotional things that start to come out; people can't
> decide from one day to the next who is my friend and who is not; what
> is the criteria that makes them my friend. There is a lot of that kind of
> stuff. (Teacher interview, October 15)

One of the insights of this study was that the cross-cultural students
who were able to make friends with those who had an established circle of
friends were then able to join that circle and not feel excluded. With Carina,
one of the most outgoing personalities in the classroom, with a large circle of
friends, initiated contact on the first day at school. For Carina, that opened
all sorts of doors, both social and linguistic. Raina's assigned friend, on the
other hand, was chosen in good faith because of her calm nature and sweet
disposition; however, she herself was not very outgoing or eager to initiate
help for Raina, nor did she have a larger circle of friends to whom Raina
could relate. It is unclear why Raina did not reciprocate the advances of the
other girls on the playground or when going down to the lunchroom. Having
more friends was such a priority for her that the reason must have been very
powerful (e.g., often the best friend of Raina's upstairs neighbor was a member of the group that was urged to invite Raina to lunch).

Students in class take their cue not only from the cross-cultural student
but also from the teacher as to how the cross-cultural student should be
treated. In this study, students seeing the lead of their teacher helping Erik, of
leaving Yevgeny alone, of having a slightly laissez-faire attitude toward Raina
were apt to follow suit. This is not to say that the teachers were not well
intentioned; it is simply to say that the teacher became a model for the rest of
the class.

The cross-cultural students responded, then, to the social interaction
early in the adjustment to school. When Raina received minimal or frustrated
responses to her initiatives, she withdrew into herself more. When Yevgeny
found that he did not have to interact, he did not, except with his Russian-
speaking translator or ESL friend. When Carina was able to take the initiative
on the playground with Mary and was warmly received, Carina's response was
also positive. Erik was constantly being helped by groupmates and classmates.

AT THE END OF THE SECOND MONTH, THE INTERVIEW WITH MRS. POPOVA HAD
started with the usual question of how the previous month had been:

Mrs. Popova: I think it has been a real tough month because Raina has now realized that there is a language barrier; she can't integrate with the kids. She was hoping that it wouldn't be so, that they could get together, but this month has shown Raina that it is not very easy and she is not part of the class yet, so she has had a month of despair. It has been a real bad month. She has felt so isolated . . .

JBC: What is the emotion she feels now?

Mrs. Popova: (in English) I think she is not happy. She is worried about this; she is not happy in the class. . . . She plays only with one or two children; not with every child, everybody. I don't know why she can't play with everybody. (Parent interview, November 10)

While this comment was being made by Mrs. Popova directly to me in English, Raina had been asked the question directly by the translator. Raina's response:

I feel angry.

When asked if Raina was angry at the teachers as well as at the children, Mrs. Popova responded that Raina was angry at the teacher because the teacher had corrected something that was correct in Bulgarian but wrong in English because of different mathematical conventions. Also, Raina was upset that the teacher had used such a "severe tone of voice" when she asked Raina about the autobiographical chapter.

Raina, as well as the other three cross-cultural students in this study, arrived with a full reservoir of high expectations and hopes. They were all very excited about the prospect of living in the United States; they all wanted to become a part of the class immediately. After approximately four days, after the terror of being in a place where they could not communicate had subsided, the students seemed to settle in and to continue with anticipation. In the face of overwhelming odds, their resiliency and eagerness returned as they tried to stay engaged in class. Time and again, as seen in their stories, the students tried to be a part of their context as best they could, whether it was learning names quickly, watching the teacher eagerly, participating in math, or practicing numbers.

However, it is noteworthy that all four students also experienced a dip in this feeling of high expectation. Even Erik, who seemed to adjust most easily, had a period of letdown about six weeks into the school year: He felt sad and frustrated that he was unable to explain himself. For Carina, her mother noticed a marked difference in her behavior at home; Yevgeny and Raina had interviews and behaviors that reflected resignation in their demeanor and attitudes. All four families reported a very difficult second month. There is psychological dislocation that occurs when one leaves all that is familiar (Eisenbruch, 1988). The disruption in the sense of selfhood and in the understanding of one's surroundings were important factors in the students' adjustment, but could be moderated with positive interactions in the receiving community. For three of the children, there was an upswing around the beginning of the third month. Raina's did not come until later in the third month, according to her teachers, although according to her, even then life was not yet better. Her reservoir of hope and high expectations had run totally dry; there had been nothing in her experiences that could nourish or fill it.

In answer to what the biggest factor was in her child's ability to learn English, Mrs. Popova said,

> Meeting with other English speakers. I think that everyday she listens to English, tries to speak with children, studies English in ESL; everyday she has homework, we get books from the library, she studies English for a long time everyday. She watches TV—I don't like this very much, but I think for her and for me, this is a help. (Parent interview, November 10)

About the middle of the third month, DebbieAnn reported that for the first time, Raina had indicated that she preferred staying in class to finish her work on the bridge project than to go to ESL. Permission was obtained from the ESL teacher, and Raina continued the process of building the bridge with toothpicks. DebbieAnn felt that it had been a real breakthrough: "Perhaps this is the key, to have small groups like this, in informal settings." She went on to say that small groups worked well for these students in math, too. It was for the sake of the whole class that she would shift to this type of teaching more frequently.

During the tenth week of classes, Raina came in from ESL while the math class was in groups. She did not have a scowl on her face; she tried to ask her deskmate what was going on or what he was doing. She walked over to peer over Marsha's shoulder to try to figure out what was happening. Finally, as a last resort, she went to DebbieAnn, who took her over to one of the large groups, put her at the opposite end from Marsha, and told two boys to help her catch up with the correcting. They were eager to and showed her their books; she took a "correcting pen" out of Josh's hand to correct her own. Without complaint, Josh went and found another. After the group had finished and dispersed, Raina went back and tried to help her deskmate with the problem he was having; she soon found that she had not yet corrected two pages in her own workbook and set about correcting those. As the students were getting ready for the next period, DebbieAnn told me that the previous day there had been another incident coming back from lunch involving the same boy using the same tone of voice, which was again misinterpreted. DebbieAnn told him it must stop; she spoke with Raina at the end of the day, telling her that if it happened again, Raina was to let her know.

At the beginning of the twelfth week, desks had been moved around again, and Raina was at the end of a group of five girls. Following the teacher's general directions, the group passed their papers to a designee, who happened to be Raina, who put them in the appropriate box. The teacher's directions were supplemented by simpler words from the four other girls, some of which could have sounded "severe," but were basically loud. When the teacher instructed one person from each group to put back the correcting pens, that also was Raina's job. After this, the class got into the discussion of the order of mathematical procedures abbreviated to PEMDAS (Parentheses, Exponents, Multiplication, Division, Addition, Subtraction). Raina was not able to follow along; I pulled up a chair and drew symbols next to the acronym she had copied from the board. The group was to practice this order by doing some problems together. Raina was able to contribute to the group process, now that she understood it. The group was to hand in their work, with the names of the members of the group; Raina leaned over as hers was written, and the author then gave the page to her to check the spelling.

In her interview at the end of the twelfth week of school, Raina was able to answer simple questions about the weekend in English. She had gone to a big Thanksgiving party with Bulgarian friends. Everyone had brought some part of a traditional Thanksgiving dinner, except for dessert, which was chocolate pie. On Saturday, she had gone to a Bulgarian friend's birthday party. When asked what she liked to do on weekends, she said that her favorite activity was to go to malls with her parents.

Asked how school was now, she answered, "Good." It was not easy yet, because she did not speak the language, but she felt she was progressing. Asked if things were better since the various incidents she had reported, she replied,

> The children seem to be behaving more normally, [and in chorus] at first they all laughed at me, but they don't now. (Student interview, December 4)

My final question that day was what she thought of schools in the United States, now that she had been here almost three months. Her response:

> They start earlier [age-wise] here. (Student interview, December 4)

During writing period in the thirteenth week of school, the students were correcting the responses they had written to some map work questions completed the previous night. Raina had forgotten to bring her map from home. As I sat next to her and she started verbalizing the responses, she began to discover that she was correct. We went ahead of where the class was so that she could have time to formulate the answer in English; she raised her hand and twice was called on for the correct answer. DebbieAnn praised her; Raina looked pleased. The following day, during an interview with the teachers, DebbieAnn said that Raina had brought in the map with as much completed on it as could be expected.

IN THE FINAL INTERVIEW, DEBBIEANN COMMENTED ON RAINA'S PROGRESS during the previous three weeks:

> You know, this is my fourth year here and every year I have had students who have come from Soviet bloc countries, and she is, by far, the most unresponsive in terms of people making advances of friendship toward her. I don't want to be unfair and say that the kids have been just blessedly wonderful, because they certainly haven't . . . but they do put forth. . . . Even today, in computer lab, she and Marsha were having a nice exchange, which was good to hear. . . . Marsha, who is usually not very animated at all . . . was very excited and animated. Raina was very deadpan during the whole thing.
>
> I think that sometimes that is really hurting her; like today . . . in a group . . . when she is there, she is not exactly invited in, but she is not excluded, she does not even join then. . . . Even as she acquires more language, she is not engaging so much. . . . She is not acclimating in the same way I have seen other students. . . . She seems very nervous much of the time and really not very happy. (Teacher interview, December 10)

DebbieAnn went on to speak briefly of extenuating factors—that she had recently become aware of the continuing tension in the relationship between the two families who shared the apartment building. Although the daughter of the upstairs neighbor was in the different section of the sixth grade, negative feelings were spilling over to the daughter's friends [one of whom stood next to Raina in chorus]; neighbor relationships were having an impact on the relationships not only at home but also at school.

Another of DebbieAnn's concerns was that Raina was no longer coming in on time. She did not know the reason for this; perhaps it was just that the beginning of school was so casual that she thought she didn't need to be there until 9:00, or perhaps it was because her mother was having problems dropping her off on time. When I asked Raina about this, she answered that she did not think that school started until 9:00. Because everyone could read whatever they wanted to for those first fifteen minutes, she assumed that that time period was not part of the school day.

DebbieAnn indicated that the blank look of which she had spoken the previous month had mostly disappeared:

> She was cute today during math. We have started geometry. She did last night's homework and . . . I said, "Problem number three." She raised her hand, which is maybe only the third time that has happened. So I was quite excited. So I said, "Raina". And she read her answer. First of all, when I [called her name] the kids all sort of looked, and then when she actually said, "Four triangles," the whole class — Maybe that is what they need to see more. And they need to see that she is not . . . without intelligence. . . . They think that because a person can't communicate, maybe they are not intelligent or can't speak. I try to accentuate that whenever I can; for example, when we are talking about following directions, I keep telling the kids that she follows directions better than they do, even though she does not understand the language. . . . Maybe I'm having unrealistic expectations. . . . Maybe if you came back in March, I would forget that up until December I felt that this poor child was totally sad all the time. (Teacher interview, December 10)

In the final interview with Mrs. Popova, she felt that Raina was trying to understand the children more now than she had been and therefore things seemed to be a little better. That thought echoed the teacher's on the previous day:

> For her, the past two weeks, I have started to see a turn around in her affect a little more. . . . [There is] definitely more involvement, more participating in class—if she has a question, I have noticed her talking to Rachel and Ann, for example. . . .There is none of this looking at me. . . . That, I think, has really improved a lot. (Teacher interview, December 10)

Even into her last interview, and in one of her last journal entries, Raina was still having problems with peer relationships. The girl who lived upstairs and her friend were making life difficult not only at home, but also at school. An entry in mid-November in response to something that made her laugh: "I don't remember anything specific that made me laugh"; in early December in response to something special that had happened: "Nothing very special has happened to me so far." Raina's wish list:

> I wish I had more friends and I could learn the language faster. I wish I could do some sports. I wish my classmates were nicer to me; for instance, that Lisa did not make faces at me or that others did not avoid me, etc. I wish the teachers could give us less homework. I wish my family bought me a little dog. (Student journal, November 17)

The Little Golden Key

The Caterpillar and Alice looked at each other for some time in silence: at last the Caterpillar . . . addressed her in a languid, sleepy voice.

"Who are you?" said the Caterpillar.

This was not an encouraging opening for a conversation. Alice replied, rather shyly, "I—I hardly know, sir, just at present—at least I know who I was when I got up this morning, but I think I must have been changed several times since then."

"What do you mean by that?" said the Caterpillar sternly. "Explain yourself!"

"I can't explain myself, I'm afraid, sir," said Alice, "because I'm not myself, you see."

"I don't see," said the Caterpillar.

"I'm afraid I can't put it more clearly," Alice replied very politely, "for I can't understand it myself to begin with; and being so . . . different . . . is very confusing."

—Lewis Carroll, Alice in Wonderland

IN OUR INCREASINGLY MULTICULTURAL WORLD, CHILDREN'S JOURNEYS INTO wonderland will grow exponentially. Teachers at all levels of education in the United States today are looking out on more diverse student populations than ever before, and will continue to do so. The diversity is composed not only of those from other lands, but also from within the borders of this country. The four stories presented in this book provide insights that can be shared across the diversity, that can become the little golden key that opened up Wonderland for Alice.

The responsibility of the host community in the adjustment of these four children cannot be overemphasized. The role of the school (the term used here as a symbol of the total community of teachers, administrators, peers, programs) in enabling cross-cultural children to acculturate is vital. While children will obviously deal with issues according to the constellation of factors that constitute their unique approaches, schools must understand the issues so that the children are not alienated and thereby driven to separation. The aim of this book is to help sensitize teachers and administrators and parents to the issues that cross-cultural students face; the following suggestions point to some of the complex areas that need to be addressed.

The Administration

The impact of the leadership of the school, particularly the principal and the mainstream teachers of cross-cultural students, is extremely important. For most cross-cultural students, school is the place of primary (and sole) contact with authority in the majority culture. It is here that cross-cultural students get an understanding not only of the language and necessary classroom behaviors, but also of the attitudes of the larger society. As a microcosm of the larger society, school is the place where students and their families become acquainted with the possibilities that lie in the future. Leadership which engenders widespread and authentic appreciation of diversity throughout its constituency (systemwide or schoolwide) enables cross-cultural students to flourish despite their lack of language.

Moreover, an understanding of the importance of the ESL or bilingual program needs to be explored with the administration (of the school or the system). Too often, because of small groupings of students, which are common to ESL programs, classes are put into overworked passageways, large closets, reverberating cafeterias, noisy locker rooms, or other discarded space; classrooms are moved mid-year; substitutes are not obtained if the regular ESL teacher is absent; criteria for hiring ESL teachers are compromised; and budgets are cut with little consideration of the ramifications for the students and the mainstream teachers. These practices reflect the priorities of the leadership. Practices that would seldom be considered for children in other special programs of the school are used too frequently in ESL programs.

As more and more cross-cultural students are being placed directly into mainstream classes, it behooves the system to provide the teachers and principals with further support: (1) In-service meetings to educate and support the mainstream teachers in strategies that help the cross-cultural student integrate into the classroom, in the cultural kinds of issues these students are dealing with, and in the process of second language learning would give the teachers confidence in their approach to the students. Alternatively, (2) a single individual, such as a cultural adjustment counselor, could bridge the gap between the cross-cultural student, mainstream teacher, and ESL teacher and provide in-class modeling and help in the mainstream classroom, particularly in the first few months of adjustment.

The ESL Program

The students profiled in this book were in ESL programs, not bilingual programs, either by default or by parental choice. These programs were a lifeline for the students and a life saver for many of the teachers. These case studies point to a larger truth: Coss-cultural students urgently need the linguistic and affective support of these programs. The need is the greatest with newcomers at the *very* beginning of the school year, in a structured, regular schedule that will help the students integrate into their classrooms. This is said with the understanding that often ESL programs cannot be fully operational until all of the schedules of all the mainstream teachers are known, so that an ESL schedule may be created. It is said with the knowledge that ESL teachers labor under overwhelming expectations and low priority (as reflected in budget cuts) in most school systems. It is said also, however, with the understanding that during those first few days and weeks, the students need the understanding and support of the ESL program the most, and in addition to all the other pressures and responsibilities that the mainstream teachers face, they cannot devote the amount of time cross-cultural students need at the beginning of the year. The cross-cultural students need the support of the ESL program early for cognitive as well as for affective purposes; they need it to help keep up their high expectations as well as to begin to learn the language. It is ironic, perhaps, that being out of the mainstream classroom will help the cross-cultural students integrate more quickly into it. This is because the skills, language, and cultural information they receive in their ESL classes are of paramount importance to that integration. At this point, the ESL program is not a "support" program, but the only viable life-line for these cross-cultural students. Later, as the students get their bearings, it can become the support program it is often called.

Even as administrators must become aware of the ways in which they treat those involved in ESL (teachers, students, program), so must those in ESL education continue their responsible advocacy on behalf of appropriate education for these children. Often the ESL teacher is the person closest to the cross-cultural student and family and has more of an understanding of the issues that confront the family. However, too often that person can resort to patching up the program instead of eliminating systemic glitches or problems that relegate the ESL students to a lesser education.

Furthermore, contact between the ESL and the mainstream teacher cannot be left to haphazard meetings. To help the student and to help the mainstream teacher, the ESL teacher must be free (and permitted) to observe in the classroom and meet with the teacher on a regular basis, until the student is able to express him- or herself fully. Many mainstream teachers will not take the initiative to make that contact. The contact must be built in systemically, in order to be of most benefit to teacher and student alike. Alternatively, a cultural adjustment counselor could be this bridge.

An informational session for parents of children in the ESL program prior to or very early in the school year would be very beneficial. Parents need to know the basic expectations of the system of education in the United States, specific expectations of a particular school or classroom, the process of second language acquisition their children will be experiencing, and their role in all of these. Some of the parents in this study suggested formulation of a booklet that would address these issues, to help the adjustment of cross-cultural students as well as their families.

The Mainstream Teacher

As important as the ESL program is, it is in the mainstream teacher's class that the cross-cultural student will spend the greater portion of time. Already overburdened by what is increasingly expected of them, mainstream teachers have varying responses to the presence of cross-cultural students in their classes. Some work very hard in conjunction with the ESL teacher; some wash their hands of the challenge without even trying; others feel that since English is their native language, ESL students should not present a linguistic challenge they cannot handle. Experience has shown that often good mainstream teaching can be sensitive to many cross-cultural issues, just as good multicultural teaching is good for *all* students.

Conscious and unconscious attitudes held by a teacher, particularly with regard to the value of the cross-cultural student to the class (or presence in the country, for that matter), affect interactions with that student. Students who are seen as a burden, as having deficiencies that must be corrected, as a drain on the teachers' time, as objects to be talked about instead of children to be talked with—attitudes such as these will become evident despite words that may try to indicate the contrary.

In the observations and interviews with the teachers in this study, a lot of their ideas, actions, and questions seemed to arise out of an unfamiliarity with the fields of cross-cultural awareness and second language acquisition. A basic understanding of the types of cultural issues and the process of second language acquisition would give the teachers a more secure base for their very well meaning strategies. Many off-hand comments indicated that the teachers were, consciously or not, uncomfortable with having an ESL student in the class simply because they were not sure of "what to do with them." Comments from teachers about their use of "stilted English," linguistic production expected too soon, compliments offered in language that was too complex, unawareness of the intense concentration required (and hence a breather now and then) in the first few weeks of school, all indicated a lack of familiarity with the particular issues of cross-cultural students. This lack of information led to reticence on the teachers' part. The high personal expectations of the teachers became thwarted, which, in turn, influenced their further attempts with the cross-cultural students.

The ways in which cross-cultural children may be different from their peers in the classroom are not all visible. Values that run deep within the culture represented by the student have already been enculturated into the child. Many such values were evident in this study. Major areas, such as learning styles, writing styles, and world views, as well as more minor ones are all shaped by culture. Our emphasis on individuality in this society is expressed in numerous ways; in Brazil, the emphasis is on the larger society (the teachers, the school), as noted by Carina's mother's description of school priorities in Brazil. Culture is not just the unique, quaint ways of other people; all people are products of their own learned and shared behaviors. Like the proverbial fish in the water, however, we have difficulty in identifying our own context, our own modus operandi until we are sensitized to it by those who hold a different gestalt. It is of utmost importance to be aware that, even in children, enculturation of their own cultural values has already taken place.

In this book, one of the mainstream teachers divided the responsibility for the cross-cultural student as 75/25 percent, the mainstream teacher having the greater share. Other mainstream teachers did not give an actual percentage, but expressed the feeling that because the student was in ESL only one hour per day, the majority of the responsibility was theirs. Mainstream teachers need to understand what it means to "own" the responsibility they claim for the cross-cultural student as a member of their class. In so doing, they need to understand what this entails, how to undertake the responsibilities associated with being so entrusted, and whom to turn to for assistance. These responsibilities would include, among others, the use of appropriate strategies for teaching, strategies that help integrate the student as quickly as possible, strategies that allow for different modalities as well as learning styles, materials that are within the student's capabilities. Understandably, this would not be possible for all subjects (e.g., the drug resistance program), but a variety of options could be explored for other subjects with the ESL teacher or other colleagues.

Great care must be exercised to understand clearly the ramifications of the inclusion of all students. Equity (of opportunity) and equality (of treatment) must not be confused to produce the exclusion of those children with linguistic issues. In the classroom, as in life, there are those who will need some extra help to understand the lesson. This help can come from the teacher, an aide, or especially, from peers, but the help *must* come so that the cross-cultural student may be given a chance to participate as early and as fully as possible. Dreeben (1968) points out that school is the place where children begin to see themselves in relation to their peers instead of their siblings and begin to assume that all peers should be treated equally. In a situation with cross-cultural students, the opportunity arises to help the mainstream students realize that *fair* is not the same as *equal*. To insist that all children be treated equally (the same) might deny some children the possibility of getting their sails up to catch the wind.

In the first few days of this study, the cross-cultural students simply wished for acknowledgment of their presence. (One child had even prepared, in advance in *very* simple English, a brief summary about his native country, but was never asked to give it.) In the first few weeks, they needed individualized attention, particularly because they did not understand what was being said to the whole class. After the students have made the initial adjustment to the class, after even the first three months, the teacher could then take their lead about how much attention they need. During their first few weeks, these students did not have the ability to make that judgment alone. Their primary focus was to survive and for that, they needed help. These are not the same issues that native-born students have, yet the teachers, unaware, used strategies similar to those used with children who are familiar with the cultural values and the language.

Cross-cultural students, like all students, have the universal need of affirmation, particularly to expedite their participation. For them, as for others, the ability to help someone else is always a great boost to the ego. Being able to show competence despite linguistic reticence enabled them to be viewed more positively by their peers. Yevgeny was asked to help younger children with jumprope activities. For someone who had been on the receiving end, on the not-knowing end of the spectrum for such a long time, this little request produced a great change for the better in his acculturation process. This is why it was such a shame that Yevgeny and Carina were not able to participate in the reading program for first-graders.

An acknowledgment of the student's strong desire to integrate into the classroom and do what the others are doing indicates the need for a closer connection between the mainstream and ESL teachers. This collaboration would also facilitate the social adjustment of the student, since often ESL teachers see a totally different child (i.e., more relaxed, happier) in their room than the mainstream teachers see in theirs. It is important to have multiple perspectives on the students in order to get a true picture.

Parents in this study suggested a buddy system a little different than "assigning a friend." Their idea was that the buddy should be someone who volunteered and that it could start before the school year began, if the children happened to be around. There was also some interest by the parents in having a family from the school that might be mentors for the cross-cultural family in their adjustment to living in the United States.

Additionally, the orientation of cross-cultural students to the school, itself, needs to be taken more seriously. One student did not know what subjects were studied in class other than math and English; another was not shown the bathroom until the end of the first day, at the request of the mother.

The Student

One of the questions that arises frequently among teachers is the issue of a perceived difference in attitude between immigrants and sojourners. In this book, the two children who adjusted most easily were sojourners; the immigrants had more difficulty. There are a variety of commonly held assumptions derived from practice about the reasons one group may adjust more easily than another: Immigrants know they are here to stay and hence must make the adjustment quickly and permanently; sojourners are here for a short period of time and do not experience the distress of having conflicting value systems for an extended time, and therefore adjust more quickly. Immigrants hold on to their culture (and language) in order to maintain their identity and do not adjust as quickly; sojourners are here for a "holiday" and feel they don't need to learn the language or the culture if staying for such a short period of time. This study supports the literature that suggests that initial adjustments are shared by both the sojourner and immigrant; length of stay for sojourner or immigrant does not seem to affect the process of the adjustment (Berry et al., 1988; Brislin, 1981; Ellingsworth, 1985; Grove and Hansel, 1982). It was a constellation of other causes that affected the adjustment, not the length of or reason for their stay.

The Approach

> The Unicorn looked at [Alice] with an air of the deepest disgust.
> "What-is-this?" he said at last.
> "This is a child!" Haigha replied eagerly, coming in front of Alice to introduce her . . . "We only found it to-day. It's as large as life, and twice as natural!"
> "I always thought they were fabulous monsters!" said the Unicorn. "Is it alive?"
> "It can talk," said Haigha, solemnly.
> The Unicorn looked dreamily at Alice, and said "Talk, child."
> Alice could not help her lips curling up into a smile as she began: "Do you know, I always thought Unicorns were fabulous monsters, too! I never saw one alive before!"
> "Well, now that we *have* seen each other," said the Unicorn, "if you'll believe in me, I'll believe in you. Is that a bargain?"
>
> —Lewis Carroll, *Through the Looking Glass*

Myths, prejudices, and fantasies are all washed away with the cleansing experience of this meeting between two who thought the other was unreal. C.S. Song (1984) has the following insight: Alice had believed *that* unicorns were monsters; now she was willing to believe *in* one. Believing *in*, which comes from the heart, is very different from believing *that*, which comes from the head. A belief *in* signifies a commitment to that person or idea; believing *that* signals that the belief can be changed or rejected. From two totally different backgrounds, Alice and the Unicorn came face to face and were willing to admit to the commonality of their both being alive. Celebrating with plum cake, the Lion, the White King, Alice, and the Unicorn accepted each other's reality as valid.

This incident from *Through the Looking Glass* speaks to the impact that personal contact has to dispel the stereotypes and prejudices we hold. While it usually does not happen as serendipitiously as for Alice and the Unicorn, it is a powerful tool that mainstream teachers of cross-cultural students have access to. This is one of the major aims of multicultural education: the exploding of myths, stereotypes, and prejudices. Multicultural education is not just having students from different ethnic backgrounds in the class; it is not just having a day for heroes or holidays, for culinary creations or costumes; it is not just having a unit on Japan or Africa as part of the curriculum. Part of multicultural education is content, yes, but it is, more urgently, an approach that can pervade all subject matter, all teaching strategies, all learning, all of schooling. It is an approach that is beneficial for all children, that searches for equity for all students, that seeks to educate all learners in decision making and problem-solving skills, that validates all heritages. It is an approach that seeks to demolish the myth of fabulous monsters and to promote belief in each other across lines of ignorance and prejudice. The reality of global, intercultural contact in our schools and in our world cannot be ignored any longer; to wish it otherwise is to miss out on the richness, the vitality, the strength it has to offer. To leave students unprepared for this reality is to fail them in one of the most crucial issues of our day.

To accomplish this task, new attitudes and approaches are required. Four of them are discussed here. First, to acknowledge differences is urgent. People talk about issues that are of importance. Therefore, what we do *not* talk about also sends a message. As Vivian Paley has pointed out in her book, *White Teacher*, many teachers believe that if they ignore differences, that is, if they are "colorblind" in their treatment of children, the differences will be diminished. However, to ignore that which is a difference also says that those differences do not amount to much—when, indeed, they do. Being of a particular ethnic or cultural background is a part of the child's identity. The child has been brought up with the values and attitudes and interactional patterns important within that group. The myriad processes by which we come to have our identities and to hold to our beliefs begin with our families. To *not* notice the way in which these factors have played an important role in the child's heritage is to not see or accept the child for who she or he really is. When one's heritage is validated all around, as happens with the dominant culture, talking about issues of identity and differences therein may seem unimportant or irrelevant. However, to have one's difference *positively* acknowledged when one is in the minority is to celebrate one's identity. In that celebration and acceptance, the cross-cultural students then become liberated to understand and/or accept aspects of the majority culture, should they wish to.

Second, there is a need to recognize the positive impact of the differences within the classroom. The assumption in many classrooms tends to be that "different is deficient." This deficit theory uses only the majority culture's yardstick as a measure, without allowing for the contributions that non-majority children bring from their backgrounds. Their experiences, while different in content, have still contributed to their development and can be used in expanding their education. As Heath (1983) pointed out in her study in the Piedmont Carolinas, all children have established means of interaction within their families. In two of the communities in her study, the interactions had a different basis and format than in the dominant majority (which was reflected in what was expected in schools). When teachers are able to incorporate aspects of the culture brought by the cross-cultural students, learning increases significantly.

The deficit theory applies to many aspects of classroom life—for example, to our expectations of parental involvement. When the parents do not show the type of interest we expect, we think they are not interested in their child's education, which is judging them by *our* standards. There may be many significant reasons why the parents do not exhibit typical Anglo-American behavior; they may express support of their child in totally different ways.

Furthermore, the assumption in the deficit theory often is that the cross-cultural students are the ones who need to do all the learning. Having this opportunity for *mainstream* students to see the world through different eyes is often overlooked. Learning to work with diversity, to celebrate it, to call on it (in the very composition of the class) for strength, imagination, and interest are vital messages to convey to mainstream students. Cross-cultural students can make a very positive contribution to a class, with or without a common language. Not only can they share their perspectives, their histories, and their lives, but they can be catalysts for having a class examine itself, its practices, its values, and its attitudes. Discussion of these topics or of the differences in perceptions can strengthen the class. Continuing to pass on society's worn-out monocultural norms will not be sufficient in this new day of multicultural explosion.

Third, some conflict is inevitable and can be very healthy, particularly if the teacher can use it as a jumping-off point for legitimate discussion. Two types of conflict arose during this study: In one, mainstream students readily excluded those who were different. These instances certainly allowed for teachable moments, at least, for the topic of tolerance. In the other type, there were times when behaviors or attitudes of cross-cultural students represented differing socializations. As secondary socializers, schools reflect in their own way the values of the dominant society. Teachers also add their implicit methods of accomplishing tasks and generating meaning in their classrooms. As cultural entities, the school and the cross-cultural student may clash in their expectations of what is defined as appropriate behavior. The clashes cannot be totally avoided—neither student nor teacher can know all that is necessary about each other's culture—but the approach to and attitude toward conflict is crucial. When conflict can be used to learn about one's own culture, when it can be approached as a look at the possible varieties of examining or solving a problem, when it can be addressed as a possible way of understanding another's viewpoint without having to accept it, when it can be appreciated as a way of learning about ideas complementary to each other instead of canceling out each other, it is beneficial indeed. It is often through conflict that we learn the values on which we base our lives and the ways our culture has shaped us.

Fourth, the pervasiveness of ecological sensitivity was enviable in the profiled schools. This can and must become true for multicultural sensitivity as well. Mainstream teachers already have an enormous task of fitting in all subject matter they need to in their day with the children. However, the definition of multicultural education as an approach as opposed to just content matter means that simple acts, here and there, can be used to expand the children's horizons even further: Pointing out a country on a map can generate interest or discussion; current events discussions can focus occasionally on places outside the United States; celebrations of differences can be extended beyond gustatory treats; opportunities to discuss ways of respecting others who are different can be explored at all levels; ways in which a cross-cultural student and the class might affect each other, even nonverbally, can be explored with the students, different learning styles can be accommodated for the benefit of all. Facility of the cross-cultural student in the language does not need to be a pre-requirement for the mainstream students to benefit from his or her presence in class. All of these ideas can be incorporated as teachable moments. The importance of simple signs of encouragement from peers and teachers alike and other ways to make the student feel welcome can be stressed, as well as the idea that communication is more than language. Just as there is a formal program in many elementary schools that educates and sensitizes abled students to the particular circumstances faced by people with disabilities, native-born children could be sensitized to the feelings of exclusion due to cultural or linguistic differences. In some situations, where bicultural students (those who are truly bicultural, not just recently arrived) have not experienced support of their ethnicity and therefore want to blend into the mainstream as much as possible, this may be a tricky topic to address. However, as teachers we cannot afford to hide in safe, calm harbors; we must help equip students with the skills and attitudes necessary for their future.

THE CHILDREN WHO ARE THE SUBJECTS OF THIS BOOK HAVE TOLD THEIR STORIES of joy and pain, of expectation and disappointment, of confusion and clarity, of excitement and disillusionment; they have shared their lives and their dreams. In the end, however, the true solution is a reciprocal equation: If children in the United States are to be adequately educated for life in the twenty-first century, they need to be acculturated to a global world. Then, all participants—newcomers, teachers, peers, parents, community—can hope, like Alice, that the dream had been shared:

> "Now, Kitty, let's consider who it was that dreamed it all. This is a serious question, . . . [The Red King] was part of my dream, of course—but then I was part of his dream, too!" (Lewis Carroll, *Through the Looking Glass*)

Glossary

Acculturation—Both a state and a process for a newcomer to live without undue stress, with satisfaction in daily activities in a new/different sociocultural setting, and with a sense of acceptance by the host culture.

Adaptation, Adjustment, Acculturation—Used interchangeably in this book.

American—This term has been avoided as much as possible, because it essentially refers to the entire western hemisphere, not just to the United States. Where possible, I have used USAmerican to appropriately narrow the focus. However, where not possible, it is used in the popular but incorrect sense, as referring to the people and majority culture of the United States of America.

Assimilation—Becoming one with the dominant society, commonly thought to be the only goal for immigrants; alternatively thought to be one of a variety of responses to the process of acculturation.

Bilingual Education—An educational approach in which students whose first language is other than English are taught subject matter in that language and they are also taught English. Home language input decreases as the students gain proficiency in English. There are many varieties of bilingual programs, differing primarily in the amount of home language and the type of translation used in the classroom.

ESL (English as a Second Language)— An educational program designed to teach English to children whose English is limited or nonexistent. Often it is part of a bilingual program. At other times, it is distinct from the bilingual program: in communities where there are not enough students of the same language background to meet the mandatory number of students for a bilingual program; or in communities where there is a very multicultural student population in need of English instruction; or in communities where parents do not opt for bilingual education for their children. In such communities, ESL programs are often the means used to teach the language to non-English speakers. These programs differ from bilingual programs in that instruction is only in English, and the ESL class population is ethnically and linguistically diverse. ESL programs themselves are based on different models; there are no mandated forms or hours the program should fulfill.

While ESL is the common terminology that is used, ESOL (English to Speakers of Other Languages) is perhaps a more apt term, even in elementary schools, as some children arrive already knowing more than one language.

The community described in this book offered both bilingual and ESL resources to the parents, who decided which program they wanted for their children. The focus of this book is how children who are in ESL programs acculturate. The ESL program in this community was based on a pull-out model, where children are taken from a mainstream class for a daily period of a minimum of an hour of ESL instruction.

NEP (Non-English Proficient) or **LEP (Limited English Proficient)**—Terms used to describe students, depending on their proficiency in English. Sometimes students are referred to as ESL students to distinguish them from NEP/LEP students who might be in bilingual programs.

Newly Arrived—For purposes of this book and the study it describes, the term means that the students had just arrived from their homelands, within a month before entering school, or that if they had arrived during the summer, that they had had no formal, structured contact with English (e.g., classes, camp, school).

References and Recommended Reading

Almy, M., and C. Genishi. 1979. *Ways of studying children.* New York: Teachers College Press, Columbia University.

Bennett, Christine. 1995. *Comprehensive multicultural education.* Boston: Allyn and Bacon.

Berry, John W., Uichol Kim, and Pawel Boski. 1988. "Psychological acculturation of immigrants." In *Cross-cultural adaptation,* edited by Y. Y. Kim and W.B. Gudykunst, 62–90. Newbury Park, CA: Sage.

Brislin, Richard. 1981. *Cross-cultural encounters.* New York: Pergamon Press.

California State University, Evaluation, Dissemination and Assessment Center. 1990. *Beyond language: Social and cultural factors in schooling language minority students.* Los Angeles. Evaluation, Dissemination, and Assessment Center.

Carroll, Lewis. *Alice in wonderland.* Kingsport, TN: Grosset and Dunlap.

Carroll, Lewis. *Through the looking glass.* Philadelphia: Henry Altemus.

Cummins, James. 1981. "The role of primary language development in promoting educational success for language minority students." In *Schooling and language minority students: A theoretical framework,* edited by CA State Dept. of Educ. Office of Bilingual Bicultural Education, 3–50. Los Angeles: Evaluation, Dissemination and Assessment Center: CSU.

Dreeben, Robert. 1968. *On what is learned in school.* Reading, MA: Addison Wesley.

137

Eisenbruch, Maurice. 1988 "The mental health of refugee children and their cultural development." *International Migration Review* 22, no. 2 (Summer): 282–300.

Ellingsworth, Huber. 1985. "The Sojourner: A Continuing source of insight about cultural entry and reentry." Conference paper, Denver, CO, November.

Florio, Susan. 1978. *Learning how to go to school: An ethnography of interaction in a kindergarten/first grade classroom.* Dissertation, Harvard University.

Gavelek, J.R. 1984. "The social contexts of literacy and schooling." In *The contexts of school-based literacy,* edited by T. Raphael, 3–26. New York: Random House.

Goodman, Mary Ellen. 1970. *The culture of childhood.* New York: Teachers College Press, Columbia University.

Grove, Cornelius Lee, and Bettina Hansel. 1982. "Two doctoral dissertations concerning the international exchange of secondary students: Reviews and critiques." *AFS occasional papers in intercultural learning,* 2.

Gudykunst, W.B., and M.R. Hammer. 1988. "Strangers and hosts: An uncertainty reduction based theory of intercultural adaptation." In *Cross-cultural adaptation,* edited by Y.Y. Kim and W.B. Gudykunst, 106–140. Newbury Park, CA: Sage.

Heath, Shirley Brice. 1983. *Ways with words.* Cambridge: Cambridge University Press.

Heath, Shirley Brice. 1986. "Sociocultural contexts of language development." In *Beyond language: Social and cultural factors in schooling language minority students,* 143–85. Los Angeles: Evaluation, Dissemination and Assessment Center: CSU.

Kimball, Solon. 1963. "Cultural influences shaping the role of the child." In *Education and culture,* edited by George Spindler, 268–284. New York: Holt, Rinehart and Winston.

Levine, Ellen. 1989. *I hate English.* New York: Scholastic Inc.

Longstreet, W. 1978. *Aspects of ethnicity.* New York: Teachers College Press.

Nieto, Sonia. 1992. *Affirming diversity.* New York: Longman.

Paley, Vivian. 1979. *White teacher.* Cambridge, MA: Harvard University Press.

Rogoff, B. 1986. "Adult assistance of children's learning." In *The contexts of school-based literacy,* edited by Terry Raphael, 27–42. New York: Random House.

Schieffelin, B., and E. Ochs. 1986. *Language socialization across cultures.* Cambridge: Cambridge University Press.

School Situations Picture Stories. 1974. In *Cultural democracy, bicognitive development, and education,* by M. Ramirez and A. Castaneda. New York: Academic Press.

Song, C.S. 1984. "The seven stages of dialogical conversion." In *Tell us our names,* 121–141. Maryknoll, NY: Orbis Books.

Spindler, G. 1974. "The transmission of culture." In *Education and the cultural process,* edited by G. Spindler, 279–310. New York: Holt, Rinehart and Winston.

Staton, Ann Q. 1990. *Communication and student socialization.* Norwood, NJ: Ablex.

Sung, Betty Lee. 1987. *The adjustment experience of Chinese immigrant children in New York City.* New York: Center for Migration Studies.

Surat, Michelle Maria. 1983. *Angel child, dragon child.* New York: Scholastic Inc.

Trueba, H. 1987. *Success or failure.* Cambridge: Newbury House.

Willett, J. 1987. "Contrasting acculturation patterns of two non–English speaking preschoolers." In *Success or failure,* edited by H. Trueba, 69–84. New York: Newbury House.

Wurzel, Jaime S. 1988. *Toward multiculturalism.* Yarmouth, ME: Intercultural Press.